The Other Poetry of Keats

The Other Poetry of Keats

by Gerald B. Kauvar

Rutherford • Madison • Teaneck
FAIRLEIGH DICKINSON UNIVERSITY PRESS

Grateful acknowledgment is made to Holt, Rinehart and Winston, Inc. for permission to quote from *Complete Poems of Robert Frost*. Copyright 1916, 1923 by Holt, Rinehart and Winston, Inc. Copyright 1944, 1951 by Robert Frost. Reprinted by permission of Holt, Rinehart and Winston, Inc.

Grateful acknowledgment is also made to Princeton University Press for permission to quote from *Aesthetic and Myth in the Poetry of Keats* by Walter Evert (Copyright © 1965 by Princeton University Press: Princeton Paperback, 1966). Reprinted by permission of Princeton University Press.

Associated University Presses, Inc.
Cranbury, New Jersey 08512

SBN: 8386 7434 8

Printed in the United States of America

To Borah and Sarah Mozer, and their daughter
Elaine, my wife

Contents

Preface

'Tis the most difficult thing in the world to me to write a preface, though there are many to whose encouragement and assistance this book owes much. I should like to try to record my debts, for proper thanks cannot be expressed. To a faculty summer fellowship from the Graduate College of the University of Illinois I am obliged for three months' time and the funds necessary to complete work on this manuscript. To William G. Lane I am indebted for first stimulating my interest in the English Romantic Poets. To Charles Nilon I owe whatever ability I have to frame the proper questions to ask about literature. To Lionel Stevenson I shall be forever in arrears; his example was no less important than his encouragement of this investigation and his confidence in my ability to pursue it.

John Cunningham, Glenn O'Malley, and Jack Stillinger read the manuscript at various stages of its preparation. Their detailed criticisms saved this book from many lapses of various kinds; those that remain are, alas, my own.

To Borah and Sarah Mozer, George Hendrick, and Ralph J. Mills, Jr., I am deeply indebted for "nameless, unremembered acts of kindness and of love," without which this book would not have existed. About my debt to my wife I can write nothing: I always made an awkward bow.

Explanatory Note

In the footnotes, the following cues refer to these major works:

Armstrong
> Armstrong, Edward A. *Shakespeare's Imagination: A Study of the Psychology of Association and Inspiration*. London, 1946.

Bate
> Bate, Walter Jackson. *John Keats*. Cambridge, Mass., 1963.

Beyer
> Beyer, Werner W. *Keats and the Daemon King*. Oxford, 1946.

Blackstone
> Blackstone, Bernard. *The Consecrated Urn: An Interpretation of Keats in Terms of Growth and Form*. New York, 1959.

Bush
> Bush, Douglas. *John Keats: His Life and Writings*. New York, 1966.

Caldwell
> Caldwell, James R. *John Keats' Fancy*. Ithaca, N.Y., 1945.

Colvin
> Colvin, Sir Sidney. *John Keats: His Life and Poetry, His Friends, Critics, and After-fame*. New York, [1917].

DeSelincourt
> DeSelincourt, E., ed. *The Poems of John Keats*. 5th ed. London, 1961,

[11

Evert

Evert, Walter. *Aesthetic and Myth in the Poetry of Keats.* Princeton, 1965.

Fausset

Fausset, Hugh I. A. *Keats: A Study in Development.* London, 1927.

Finney

Finney, Claude Lee. *The Evolution of Keats's Poetry.* 2 vols. Cambridge, Mass., 1936.

Ford

Ford, Newell F. *The Prefigurative Imagination of John Keats.* Palo Alto, Calif., 1951.

Garrod

Garrod, H. W. *Keats.* London, 1926.

Living Year

Gittings, Robert. *John Keats: The Living Year.* London, 1954.

Mask of Keats

————. *The Mask of John Keats.* London, 1960.

Lowell

Lowell, Amy. *John Keats.* 2 vols. Boston and New York, 1925.

Murry

Murry, John M. *Keats.* London, 1955.

Perkins

Perkins, David. *The Quest for Permanence.* Cambridge, Mass., 1959.

Pettet

Pettet, E. C. *On the Poetry of Keats.* New York, 1957.

Ridley

Ridley, M. R. *Keats' Craftmanship: A Study in Poetic Development.* Oxford, 1933.

Slote

Slote, Bernice. *Keats and the Dramatic Principle.* Lincoln, Nebr., 1958.

Spurgeon

Spurgeon, Caroline. *Shakespeare's Imagery and What It Tells Us*. Cambridge, 1935.

Thorpe

Thorpe, Clarence DeW. *The Mind of John Keats*. New York, 1926.

Van Ghent

Van Ghent, Dorothy. "Image Types and Antithetical Structures in the Work of Keats," Ph. D. diss., University of California, 1942.

Ward

Ward, Aileen. *John Keats: The Making of a Poet*. New York, 1963.

Wasserman

Wasserman, Earl. *The Finer Tone: Keats' Major Poems*. Baltimore, 1953.

All letters are quoted from the Rollins Edition of 1958.

Introduction

"I had not a dispute but a disquisition with Dilke, on various subjects; several things dovetailed in my mind, & at once it struck me, what quality went to form a Man of Achievement especially in Literature & which Shakespeare posessed so enormously—I mean *Negative Capability,* that is when man is capable of being in uncertainties, Mysteries, doubts, without any irritable reaching after fact & reason."

Letters, I, 193.

"This crossing a letter is not without its association—for chequer work leads us naturally to a Milkmaid, a Milkmaid to Hogarth Hogarth to Shakespeare Shakespear to Hazlitt Hazlitt to Shakespeare and thus by merely pulling an apronstring we set a pretty peal of Chimes at work."

Letters, I, 280.

"It is a wretched thing to confess; but it is a very fact that not one word I ever utter can be taken for granted as an opinion growing out of my identical nature—how can it, when I have no nature?"

Letters, I, 387.

"I am however young writing at random—straining at particles of light in the midst of a great darkness—without knowing the bearing of any one assertion of any one opinion. Yet may I not in this be free from sin?"

Letters, II, 80.

"Do not the Lovers of Poetry like to have a little Region to wander in where they may pick and choose, and in which the images are so numerous that many are forgotten and found new in a second Reading: which may be food for a Week's stroll in the Summer?"

Letters, I, 170.

". . . . all I can say is that where there are a throng of delightful Images ready drawn simplicity is the only thing."

Letters, I, 223.

"Poetry should be great & unobstrusive, a thing which enters into one's soul, and does not startle it or amaze it with itself but with its subject."

Letters, I, 224.

"Here are the Poems—they will explain themselves—as all poems should do without any comment."

Letters, II, 21.

"These lines give some insight into K's mode of writing Poetry. He has repeatedly said in conversation that he never sits down to write, unless he is full of ideas—and then thoughts come about him in troops, as tho' soliciting to be accepted & he selects—one of his Maxims is that if P. does not come naturally, it had better not come at all. the moment he feels any dearth he discontinues writing & waits for a happier moment. He is generally more troubled by a redundancy than by a poverty of images, & he culls what appears to him at the time the best.—He never corrects, unless perhaps a word here or there should occur to him as preferable to an expression he has already used—He is impatient of correcting, & says he would rather burn the piece in question & write another or something else—"My judgment, (he says,) is as active while I am actually writing as my imagination. In fact, all my faculties are strongly excited, & in their full play—And shall I afterwards, when my imagination is idle, & the heat in which I wrote, has gone off, sit down coldly to criticise when in possession of only one faculty, what I have written when almost inspired." This fact explains the reason of the Perfectness, fullness, richness & completion of most that comes from him—He has said, that he has often not been aware of the beauty of some thought or expression until after he has composed & written it down—It has then struck him with astonishment— & seemed rather the production of another person than his own."

> From Richard Woodhouse:
> Criticism of a Sonnet by Keats,
> in *The Keats Circle,* ed. Hyder
> Rollins, 2nd ed., 1965, Vol. I, 128–29.

". . . touches of Beauty should never be half way therby making the reader breathless rather than content: the rise, the progress, the setting of the imagery should like the Sun come natural to him—shine over him and set soberly although in magnificence leaving him in the Luxury of twilight."

> *Letters,* I, 238.

The primary focus of this study is on the poetry of John Keats, though not primarily on that part of the canon usually considered major. To explain, explicate, and interpret the poems is the purpose, and the technique is analysis of the expressive functioning of Keats's figurative language. Of course, the technique itself is not new, but it has never been systematically applied to the poetry with the same intentions or results.

For purposes and reasons set forth in the first chapter I have adopted a new terminology in this study: the discrete parts of figurative expressions I call "terms of a relationship," and the meanings of the terms I call "significations." Analysis of figurative relationships leads the student of Keats's poetry to several kinds of discoveries. Often the structural relevance of a sequence of images is made clear and a poem's submerged theme brought into the light. The technique I have adopted has proved to be even more useful in the analysis of groups of two or more poems that share one or more structurally important relationships. Very often the relationship itself is not immediately

obvious; we become aware of it because we recognize significations previously discovered inherent in a relationship. For example, our familiarity with Keats's notion that fancy's "silken
leash" ought to be loosed in order that the winged fancy can
bring us joy, affords us a clue to the meaning of the lyric, "I
had a dove," because we can identify the dove with fancy when
we learn

> Its feet were tied
> With a silken thread.

This identification, it should be noted, not only gives us an
insight into the lyric, but it also allows us to examine and compare the attitudes Keats held toward one of his central concerns.

Throughout this study the term "fragmented relationships"
refers to relationships that are not easily or immediately recognizable as having figurative significance. As in the example
just cited, the relationship is fragmented inasmuch as most
readers are not aware that more than one term is involved in
a complete, proper apprehension of the dove; using more conventional terminology, we do not perceive that the dove is not
an "image" but a "symbol." As I argue in more detail in part
one of the appendix, it is probably because relationships like
these are whole and familiar in Keats's mind that the poetry
presents incompletely stated, fragmented relationships. Keats
may not have been aware any more than we are—though for
different reasons—that his figurative relationships are not often
fully expressive.

As we examine and compare we shall find that frequently
poems containing a statement about or an attitude toward a
problem that vitally concerned Keats will exhibit similar relationships. By analyzing the precise significations Keats uses in
each particular instance we can discover fairly precisely the
emotional coloration in his attitudes. That Keats developed
and matured emotionally will come as no surprise, but it has
not been adequately demonstrated that we can trace in the

texture of his poems the alternations in his attitudes toward love, death, knowledge, the function of the poet, the realm of the visionary imagination, and so on. Because the problems recurred in Keats's life and thought, the images in which these thoughts were conveyed, much like an aerogramme in which writing sheet and envelope are part of a continuous whole, were similarly persistent, though their precise significations altered as Keats's feelings or thoughts altered. Because the problems and the relationships in which they achieve poetic expression were persistent, they are found to be so familiar *in toto* to the poet that often he allows them to appear synecdochically in his poetry. It is frequently necessary to examine the relationships in one poem in the light of the way in which they are used in earlier or later poetry, though never allowing any particular signification to be applied procrusteanly.

In chapter one, the technique is outlined theoretically and applied to the analysis of single poems. The technique proves capable of demonstrating structural significance, in "Hads't thou lived," and in the Chapman's *Homer* sonnet, and accounting for irony and paradox as potential structures. In chapter two, Keats's sonnet "How many bards" is given a fresh, coherent interpretation based on the analysis of its fragmented relationships in the light of their appearance and functioning in other of Keats's poems. Chapter three presents the analysis of two groups of poems exhibiting separate, fragmented relational systems, both of which reveal that Keats held—consciously or not—theories of catharsis and symbolic action. The poet-physician relationship, which loomed so large in Keats's life and poetry, is also elucidated. The focus of interest in chapter four is the nightingale ode, or, more precisely, those relationships which, stylistically achieving their happiest expression in the ode, appear in significant thematic detail in other poems. By juxtaposing the relationships and comparing the significations of the terms, we discover alternative endings to the problem of attaining and maintaining the realm of the visionary imagination; we discover two alternative answers to the question of the location of fancy's proper realm; and we discover early associations between the sexual and poetic acts of creation.

Chapter five continues the discussion begun in chapter four of the epistle to J. H. Reynolds, and explores the relationships it shares with the sonnet "To Sleep" and "Isabella," and a suggestion about the genesis of the sonnet is put forth based on these relationships. The analysis in chapter six of Keats's shifting attitudes toward the acquisition of knowledge shows him reverting to the attitude that knowledge could be gained without pain before he concludes by relating the processes of nature to the gradual ripening of the intellect. In chapter seven, the examination of Keats's attitudes toward death demonstrates that one of his earliest attitudes persisted all his life, despite his apparent rejection of easeful death in the odes, and despite his maturing philosophy of life as a vale of soul-making.

Chapter eight begins by examining the new reality for which death was temporarily rejected in the "Ode on Indolence," and after analysis of the dream sonnet and "La Belle Dame" concludes that the ode represents another attempt by Keats to frame the existence of an ideal earthly state, realistically attainable, including love, which presents a viable alternative to death. The existence of such a state is found to be denied in "La Belle Dame." Further variations on the theme of love between mortal and immortal, and the conditions of that love, are traced, and Keats's more positive conjectures or alternatives are found expressed in "Endymion" and "Unfelt, unheard, unseen." The last part of the chapter examines the relationships by which Keats expresses his views on the proper conduct for lovers, mistresses, and suitors. Chapter nine traces Keats's use of the sea as a symbol; it shows how the poet's manipulation of significations describes his movement toward and away from an ability to tolerate ambivalence.

The analysis of relationships shared by "Specimen of an Induction" and several later poems is the material of the tenth chapter. The poem is shown to be a complete poem on the subject of poetic inspiration, not the fragment it is usually considered to be. Similarly, "Calidore" is shown in chapter eleven to have as its underlying theme the growth of the poet. Chapter twelve contributes to the discussion of the authenticity of "The Poet" by analyzing in greater detail the internal evidence, especially regarding the close similarities to "Sleep and Poetry," thus adding more weight to the attribution of the sonnet to Keats. In chapter thirteen, Keats's explorations of memory's capacity for conveying pleasure, pain, or pleasureful pain are traced through two groups of poems. It is indicative of Keats's "Gordian complication of feelings" about women (*Letters,* I, 342) that analysis of the shared relationships cannot unravel his attitudes toward love, the realm of the imagination, philosophy, and death as they appear in the ode "To Fanny."

In order to show as clearly as possible Keats's changing attitudes, the chapters are organized thematically and, whenever possible, chronologically. Especially in part three, which deals with less pervasive themes, the poems are discussed in the order of their composition. Because part two deals with themes that recur constantly in Keats's life and art it has not always been possible to discuss the poetry chronologically.

I had thought of entitling this work "The Chameleon Poet," but as the phrase is used in Keats's letter of 27 October 1817 and in Robert Gittings' *The Mask of Keats* it patently refers to negative capability rather than alternations of attitudes, to philosophy and the personalities of others rather than the expression of Keats's own personality. While there is discoverable in any given attitude a basis for philosophical systematizing or an example of acting according to a determinable set of philosophical tenets, these need not be the focus of another work on Keats.[1]

---

[1] This ought not lead anyone to imagine that I am concurring with E. C. Pettet's ideas about the emphasis on "poesy" in Keats's major poetry (see his chapter ten, pp. 348–55), any more than I agree with Garrod's stress on Keats's use of the five senses (see especially p. 36).

The critical philosophy of the sort of investigation I have been describing needs some explanation, for a question that immediately asks itself is whether the investigation concerns the poet or the poem. The answer is "both," although I have attempted at all times to keep the major portion of my attention focused on the poetry.[2] I heartily agree that to read the poems as autobiography is fraught with dangers,[3] and I also agree that our judgments and estimates of the poems ought not be based on nonliterary grounds. But I do think that we can utilize information from the biography, and in this case the letters, to help us understand the poetry, provided that we do not force either the poem or the biography to conform to an artificially imposed structure of meanings. The procedure I have followed is, fundamentally, analytic: I compare shared relationships in order to determine whether Keats's poems explain each other. Supporting evidence for attitudes detected in the analysis of relationships is brought in from the sources I mentioned above, though I have rarely indulged in the luxury of interpreting relationships in the light of the ways in which they were used in other literature with which Keats may have been familiar.

It has long been recognized that the composition of poetry is a form of symbolic action,[4] and in chapter three I shall demonstrate that Keats held a similar theory. Although we shall find Keats symbolically positing alternative actions, and although he generally writes dramatically or objectively, nevertheless the mind that created the dramatic structure was

---

[2] As Kenneth Burke has stated, "Our primary concern is to follow the transformations of the poem itself. But to understand its full nature as a symbolic act, we should use whatever knowledge is available." *A Grammar of Motives,* New York, 1945, p. 451. See also Spurgeon, p. 12.

[3] Murry remarks, on p. 177, "Keats had to live all his great poems." If so, my stress would be on the word "all."

[4] "For a poem is an act, the symbolic act of the poet who made it—an act of such a nature that, in surviving as a structure or object, it enables us as readers to re-enact it." Burke, p. 447.

Keats's.[5] The dramatic mode may well have been utilized in order that he could better evaluate his attitudes by presenting them as more or less detached, objective, self-contained, self-radiant constructs.

As we trace Keats's attitudes toward both major and minor problems by means of analyzing the relationships in which they are expressed, we shall find him positing, testing, and rejecting or accepting alternative solutions. (I would prefer to say attitudes[6] or speculations, but solutions will do if we do not think of them as being necessarily logical or philosophical.) Keats tries on, as it were, several solutions; he brings them into the

---

[5] Bernice Slote comments, "The problem of whether or not to assume an autobiographical understructure for a poem becomes increasingly precarious in Keats's work. In the early poems he always seems to speak directly; in the developing body of his work he turns more and more to the dramatic voice, either a character to represent a mood, or a structure to fulfill a meaning." (p. 134.) But, as Miss Slote continues, "The use of a dramatic voice does not deny autobiographical relationships, but it implies a subtler identification by idea and theme rather than by fact." (p. 135)

The *locus classicus* of image-oriented criticism and its relation to autobiography is Caroline Spurgeon's *Shakespeare's Imagery and What it Tells Us*. Miss Spurgeon says, "I believe we can draw from the material of a poet's images definite information about his personality." (p. 12) An earlier statement discusses the dramatic mode: "In the case of a poet, I suggest it is chiefly through his images that he, to some extent unconsciously, gives himself away. He may be, and in Shakespeare's case is, almost entirely objective in his dramatic characters and their views and opinions, yet like the man who under stress of emotion will show no sign of it in eye or face, but will reveal it in some muscular tension, the poet unwittingly lays bare his own innermost likes and dislikes, observations and interests, associations of thought, attitudes of mind and beliefs, in and through the images, the verbal pictures he draws to illuminate something quite different in the speech and thought of his characters." (p. 4)

[6] Kenneth Burke finds that "As for designating of the Urn as an 'attitude,' it fits admirably with our stress upon symbolic action. For an attitude is an arrested or incipient *act*—not just an *object* or *thing*." (p. 459)

light, scrutinizes them, and in a later poem, alters, rejects, or adopts them.[7]

Quite often we shall not find Keats remaining content with the solution we would have him hold;[8] only infrequently will we find a regular stepping of the imagination toward what we might call truth or maturity. Let us say with Lionel Trilling that Keats was capable of "remaining content with contradictory knowledges,"[9] or with Bernice Slote that "Keats did accept and use his own contradictory half-knowledge."[10] But if we do, we shall be taking at face value and as final Keats's own statements on negative capability, his lack of identity, and his chameleon nature. We can, of course, recall that this essentially dramatic attitude is evident in many of his greatest poems, as Miss Slote demonstrates in her analysis of "Lamia."[11] Or we can find in the major poems evidence of a more regular stepping toward an Everlasting Yea, as Wasserman suggests at the end of his examination of those poems.[12] Yet if we examine the bulk of the poetry, especially with the order of composition in

---

[7] Albert Gérard finds that in Keats's poems "he gives a voice and an unexpected beauty to something that is specifically ours: a desperate hankering after truth, and a devastating honesty in recognizing that truth—if there be such a thing—lies beyond human reach." "Coleridge, Keats, and the Modern Mind," *EC,* I (July 1951), 261. I agree with this, but would like to enlarge the reference and say that Keats constructs and examines alternative answers to what Gérard calls "right questions," those "which are torturing us just now" (p. 260), and that he does this in successive poems as well as within single pieces.

[8] R. D. Havens' article on "Unreconciled Opposites in Keats," (*PQ,* XIV (Oct. 1935), p. 300) stresses that unfairly we tend to "remould his genius to our heart's desire" and that we are "incited to this by his rapid changes of mood and his vigorous and unqualified assertion of the truth, the aspect of life, the mood with which at the time he happened to be concerned."

[9] In "The Poet as Hero: The Letters of John Keats," *Cornhill Magazine.* CLXV (Autumn 1951), 296.

[10] Slote, p. 23.

[11] *Ibid.,* chapter 9.

[12] Wasserman, p. 223.

mind, we shall often find a rejection of a mature acceptance of a "both-and" world and reversion to an "either-or" quest for certainty.

The present study undertakes to examine closely the other poetry of Keats, that which has not received the close attention it deserves both for its own sake and for the light it sheds on Keats's development. What this study reveals is that although he retraces old concerns in a reciprocal—or alternating, irregular—manner, nevertheless his poetry is not so fully organic as is often assumed, for a sense of continual emotional development is only infrequently visible. Let me stress that his incessant self-quizzing, his constant rethinking and refeeling of human concerns, his dialogues with himself and his environment, his stubborn refusal to remain content with an attitude without testing it against a variety of circumstances, all this ought to make Keats's poetry even more relevant to our lives. Surely a century that has learned to celebrate the totality of Keats's humanity will not discard him because he is imperfect.

So the kinds of understanding generated in this study may not have any bearing on our evaluations of the poetry; they cannot alter what the poem *qua* poem is or does; but they do provide us with fresh readings of some poems, and we can afford to slough lightly no approach that concentrates on the poetry.

The Other Poetry of Keats

Part I:

Images and Relationships

[1]

Understanding Figurative Language

. . . . the investigation of metaphor is curiously like the investigation of any of the primary data of consciousness: it
cannot be pursued very far without our being led to the
borderline of sanity.

> J. M. Murry, *Countries*
> *of the Mind,* 2nd series,
> Oxford, 1931, p. 1.

Image and metaphor, simile and symbol, are not always easily
distinguishable, for each is, potentially, a figure of speech that
posits a relationship between two terms. Traditionally the classifications of figures have been based on the way in which the
relationship is presented, whether, for example, the relationship is stated or implied, on whether both terms are stated or
implied, on the frequency of a term's appearance, or on the
concreteness of the terms. Frequently the idea of comparison
is invoked in discussions of simile and metaphor, while the
notion of representation is involved in discussions of image
and symbol. There has been some attempt to define the figures
by the kind of comparison or representation involved; for example, in metonymy something closely related to a term is said
to stand for that term, while in synecdoche the part is said to
stand for the whole.

These classifications have largely overlooked the function of the figures, which is, I take it, to express a relationship between two terms. Whether the terms are simple or complex, compared or represented, concrete or abstract, there is no system of classification that begins to extract the meanings, intellectual and emotional, of the relationship in which the terms are placed in a poem. The problem is twofold: first, one must discover the qualities, properties, attributes, and meanings of each term; second, one must analyze the nature of the relationship into which the terms with their cluster of significations are placed.

Three fundamental kinds of relationships can be shown to exist. To diagram them is to understand them more easily. In what follows, the letters A and B signify the terms—in the order in which they occur in a poem—and their significations.

1.

In this first relationship, all the significations of one term are completely subsumed in those of the other term, but the reverse is not true: only part of the significations of one term are the same as those of the other. Of crucial importance is which term is subsumed.

2.

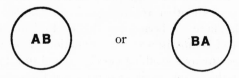

This relationship expresses identity. All the significations of one term are possessed by the other. Again the order in which the terms are mentioned is important, as is which term is the more discussed or elaborated in the poem.

3.

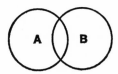   and all degrees
of union to

The diagram here represents the partial identity of significations. Order is obviously important.

The nature of the relationship expressed is often modified by what preceded it and often modifies and is modified by what follows, so that the relationship is of structural significance in poetry. What is fundamental to an understanding of poetry is that the reader understand the significations of the terms, the kind of relationship in which the terms are placed, which of the significations are shared and which are not, and the structural importance of any single signification and/or relationship.

To ground this in poetry, I should like to examine briefly Robert Frost's "Nothing Gold Can Stay."

> Nature's first green is gold,
> Her hardest hue to hold.
> Her early leaf's a flower;
> But only so an hour.
> Then leaf subsides to leaf.
> So Eden sank to grief,
> So dawn goes down to day.
> Nothing gold can stay.

The first line establishes that a relationship exists between two terms, A and B, "Nature's first green" and "gold." If we take the signification—or, rather, one of the significations—of "first green" as "beginnings," we shall not be doing violence to the particular examples of "first green" that are given in the poem. The significations of "gold" include a red-yellow color, value, rarity, and durability. The poem cites three examples of "beginnings" which, again in a certain relationship, share most but not all of these significations of "gold." It is sufficient for our purposes to notice that the quality of durability is the signification that is always absent. The poem, then, begins by stating a type 2 relationship,

but when the poem explores the relationship it is discovered to be a type 3 relationship, which looks like this:

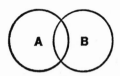

It should be noted that the poem explores most thoroughly that signification of B, durability, which is not shared by A. The initial relationship is seen to be specious and paradoxical, but this is the structural framework of the poem.

A more complex example is provided by Keats's sonnet "On First Looking Into Chapman's *Homer*." Two of the words in the first line are, in fact, terms of a relationship, a discovery that we can make only after line 6.

Much have I travell'd in the realms of gold,
    And many goodly states and kingdoms seen;
    Round many western islands have I been
    Which bards in fealty to Apollo hold.
Oft of one wide expanse had I been told
        That deep-brow'd Homer ruled as his demesne;
        Yet did I never breathe its pure serene
Till I heard Chapman speak out loud and bold:
Then felt I like some watcher of the skies
    When a new planet swims into his ken;
Or like stout Cortez when with eagle eyes
    He star'd at the Pacific—and all his men
Look'd at each other with a wild surmise
        Silent, upon a peak in Darien.

In the first line, "travell'd" is in a relationship with "reading," and "gold" is in a relationship with certain kinds of reading matter. References early in the poem to "western islands" "Which bards in fealty to Apollo hold" clarify the relationship of "gold" to reading matter, for it is likely that Greek authors— some no doubt of the Golden Age—are universally agreed to possess beauty, value, and durability. It might be argued that such books are often sumptuously bound and gilt edged.[1] But the relationship of traveling to reading does not become clear until the end of the poem. There are many ways to travel and many kinds of travelers. Some travel in an attempt to confront themselves constantly with new sights, often moving on before studying the sight they were seeing. Some travel in order to discover new experiences that can be assimilated into the core of their being. Analysis of the other relationships in the poem, the significations of splendor and royalty evoked by "states and kingdoms," "fealty," "ruled," and "demesne," and the intense sensory experiences catalogued in "breathe its pure serene," "speak out loud and bold" (which is an aural experience), and then the sharpness and vividness of the act of watching with "eagle eyes" that stare, or with eyes filled with "wild surmise," the vast scope signified by "skies," "new planet," "the Pacific," all these significations in relationship to traveling tell us that Keats's reading was of the sort that discovers personal significance in new books and that assimilates these significances into his personality. The relationship between term A, traveling, and the implied term B, reading, is

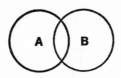

[1] Compare "Isabella,"

> Too many doleful stories do we see,
> Whose matter in bright gold were best be read.
>   II. 93–94.

and the poem explores the area AB. The appropriate significations of A are given by the sonnet in lines 6–14. In fact, it is not until line 6 that the second term is implied, though its significations have already been established in the relationship of "gold" and certain books. The whole poem explores the relationship of A, discovery—by sea voyage primarily, as suggested also when the planet "swims" into ken[2]—and B, reading classical authors, and it can be diagrammed:

Gerard Manly Hopkins' sonnet "The Caged Skylark" develops the significations of an extended simile in an effort to surprise the reader out of a stock response into new awareness. The poem's structure lulls the reader into the expectation that an initial pattern of elaborated likenesses will continue and expand throughout the sonnet.

As a dare-gale skylark scanted in a dull cage
   Man's mounting spirit in his bone-house, mean house,
      dwells—
   That bird beyond the remembering his free fells;
This in drudgery, day-laboring-out life's age.

Though aloft on turf or perch or poor low stage,
   Both sing sometimes the sweetest, sweetest spells,
   Yet both droop deadly sometimes in their cells
Or wring their barriers in bursts of fear or rage.

Not that the sweet-fowl, song-fowl, needs no rest—
Why, hear him, hear him babble and drop down to his nest,
   But his own nest, wild nest, no prison.

---

[2] Compare "Lamia,"

              his watching eyes may swim
       Into forgetfulness.
                    II. 226–27.

Man's spirit will be flesh-bound when found at best,
But uncumbered: meadow-down is not distressed
  For a rainbow footing it nor he for his bones risen.

The poem begins with two lines that tell us that man's soul constrained in his body is like a skylark "scanted in a dull cage." The first line presents the bird; the second, the man. The structural pattern continues in the quatrain: line 3 presents the bird "beyond the remembering his free fells"; line 4 elliptically pictures the drudgery of man's life.

The second quatrain describes both bird and man together: all the significations, which take the form of activity, are shared. The structure, then, may be diagrammed:

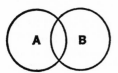 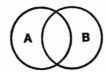

Hence, when lines 9–11 reveal the bird's need for rest after activity, rest in his natural habitat, not in a cage, we expect that lines 12–14 will similarly celebrate the joys of the released soul. Yet they do not; they specifically deny the further extension of the relationship. The poem breaks fresh ground in the last three lines. The relationship of soul is to body as bird is to cage is no longer relevant, for man's skeleton is not cage-like: The relationship between the body and the soul is not prison-like or inhibitory or destructive; rather, the two interact and combine, and the constituents and the whole are mutually enhanced in the newly presented relationship. The structure of the initial relationship as it appears at the end of the poem would be diagrammed:

The radiance, wholeness, and harmony of the final relationship between the soul and the body are intensified by the reader's simultaneous perception of the now-shattered initial relationship. Though the reader's expectations are apparently frustrated, his feelings may well be compensated by the joy and optimism of the poem's conclusion.

It may not be necessary to point out that the methodology for the analysis of figurative relationships I have just described is not at all dependent on the use of diagrams, but I should like to suggest that the diagrams have proved useful in teaching the method to college students.

TRAINS OF PEACEFUL IMAGES

Not all poetry, perhaps not even most poetry, contains relationships of such obvious structural importance. However, this method of analyzing relationships by taking account of potential significations within the terms is applicable to any poem in which such a relationship exists, no matter how obvious or minute its role may seem to be. To make literal the imaginative workings of the poem is to understand the poem better, though it cannot act as a substitute for any other interpretive strategy, much less for the poem itself. It can provide, I think, insights of scope, precision, and coherence, into single works of art and adequately deal with diverse kinds of art.[1] Examining potential significations can account for chains of images that seem weakly linked by pointing out unsuspected relationships. It can thus demonstrate new or unperceived principles of organization in poems that seem to provide, in Keats's words, little more than regions "to wander in where they [readers] may pick and

---

[1] Abrams' criteria for a "good critical theory" are "the scope, precision, and coherence of the insights that it yields into the properties of single works of art and the adequacy with which it accounts for diverse kinds of art." Meyer Abrams, *The Mirror and The Lamp* (New York, 1958), pp. 4–5. I have taken the liberty to adopt these as the criteria of successful interpretive strategies as well as good critical theories.

choose, and in which the images are so numerous that many are forgotten and found new in a second Reading" (*Letters,* I, 170). For students of Keats's early poetry this technique may establish the correctness of Croker's contention that the sound of a rhyme word and not its meaning produced Keats's series of images,[2] or it may support Jeffrey's idea that although the first word that presented itself was taken for a rhyme, that word became the germ for a new cluster of images.[3] Perhaps the technique will establish that an even more organic design informs Keats's sequences of imagery,[4] as would seem to be the

[2] See his review of "Endymion" in *Quarterly Review,* XXXVII, vii (April 1818), 204.

[3] See his review of "Endymion, Lamia, Etc." in *Edinburgh Review,* XXXIV (August 1820), 206.

[4] The difficulties inherent in this sort of investigation as it applies to Keats have been set forth by Cleanth Brooks in his comparison of Shakespeare and Donne:

> With Donne, of course, the chains of imagery, 'always vivid' and 'often minute' are perfectly evident. For many readers they are all too evident. The difficulty is not to prove they exist, but that, on occasion, they may subserve a more imaginative unity. With Shakespeare, the difficulty may well be to prove that the chains exist at all. In general, we may say Shakespeare has made it relatively easy to choose what they like and reject what they like. What he gives on one or another level is usually so magnificent that the reader may find it easy to ignore the other levels. *The Well-Wrought Urn* (New York, 1947), p. 28.

Dorothy Van Ghent discusses the problem of Keats's image series by suggesting that

> in sketching hypothetically Keats's modes of composition, one would trace the gradually more firm integration of typical image-kinds and clusters with the emotions to which they had early attached themselves as correlatives. (p. 193)

She continues:

> One would say that the passivity of the psychological process, whereas it had yielded simple chain-likeness of composition in some of his early work, yields organic modes of imagination and

case in the poem he wrote 14 February 1816, "To ****," or "Hadst thou liv'd in days of old." Not only is the poem revealed to be more fully, more poetically integrated and coherent than it is usually thought to be, but its thematic significance becomes evident through an examination of the figurative relationships.

The poem begins with a catalogue of a woman's beauties, including her bright, humid eyes

> Over which thine eyebrows, leaning,
> Picture out each lovely meaning:
> In a dainty bend they lie,
> Like to streaks across the sky,
> Or the feathers from a crow,
> Fallen on a bed of snow.
> Of thy dark hair that extends
> Into many graceful bends:
> As the leaves of Hellebore
> Turn to whence they sprung before.

The sequence overtly compares the curving of a woman's eyebrows and her wavy hair to certain natural objects that exhibit similar curvature. But it should be noticed that the various objects to which comparison is made exhibit further relationships to each other and to the woman. Clouds curving in the sky are almost always white. Feathers, which may have been suggested by a sky-bird association, not only are curved, but are texturally more similar to eyebrows than clouds are. A woman who has dark hair probably has dark eyebrows as well, and so the feather must come from a dark-plumaged bird. Crows are black, but they are also associated with carrion, with death, their color presenting a sort of natural symbolism. The importance of the last signification will become clear shortly.

---

compositional patterns, inasmuch as that passivity itself allowed these images, held enduringly in solution in his mind, a ready and intimate correlation with such affective drives as found expression in the writing of poetry. pp. 193–94.

The whiteness of the clouds—and perhaps the submerged signification of death in the bird image—may account for the
snow's being chosen to describe the whiteness of the woman's
skin. Her dark hair is compared to Hellebore in terms of grace-
ful curving, but Hellebore, in a very common species, not only
has curving leaves but also white blossoms. In fact, white
Hellebore is used medicinally to produce muscular relaxation;
it is both a sedative and a poison. Keats, having been a medical
student, might well have been aware of the plant's pharmaco-
logical properties. These significations of death, hitherto submerged, become important at the end of the poem.

The last series of comparisons is based on a Spenserian conception of the woman as knight, a sort of Britomart. It ends as
follows:

> thy sword unsheath!
> Sign of the enchanter's death;
> Bane of every wicked spell;
> Silencer of dragon's yell.
> Alas! thou this wilt never do:
> Thou are an enchantress too,
> And wilt surely never spill
> Blood of those whose eyes can kill.

The last line seems to shift the emphasis from the woman's
eyes to the eyes of others, but this change is uncalled for. If the
woman were to possess eyes that kill she would not need a
sword and the "Blood of those" would not be spilled. But if
her opponents, presumably knights since the contest is between
knights and enchantresses or enchanters, have eyes that kill,
then the line suggests that the woman loses the battle, and her
beauty, which has been the subject of the poem, is exposed as
powerless. It is possible that the "whose" in the last line might
well have been a slip of the pen written instead of "whom."
The line would then suggest that the woman has eyes to kill
those who are sensitive to beauty; she becomes a special kind
of enchantress. There is some contextual evidence for such a

reading. All four transcripts of the poem contain four additional lines:

> Ah me! whither shall I flee?
> Thou hast metamorphosed me. (1. 70)
> Do not let me sigh and pine,
> Prythee be my valentine. (1. 72)

It is the woman who metamorphoses the speaker; she changes his identity, in a sense of killing the old one. Her eyes change him, a knight, into a being enthralled by her beauty. This notion of a change from strong to weak, from knight-at-arms to wretched wight is familiar in Keats's later poetry. In "Lamia" the love of Lycius for the lamia leads to his death, and in "La Belle Dame" the knight escapes the lady whose wild eyes enthrall him, but he is incurably ill and still enthralled at the end. It is plain that the theme of love and death, or death as an aspect of love, which is so predominant in the later poetry,[5] as in "Lamia," "La Belle Dame," "Ode on a Grecian Urn," and the "Bright Star" sonnet, is adumbrated in the submerged relationships discoverable in "To ****," "Hadst thou liv'd in days of old."[6]

It is also plain that much of the rhythm and diction is flabby. Despite such textural weaknesses, "To ****" substantiates sev-

---

[5] And even in the early poetry: "Endymion," IV, 759 reads: "We might embrace and die: voluptuous thought!" This is the emotional equivalent of the sentence from the letter to Fanny Brawne of 25 July 1819, "I have two luxuries to brood over in my walks, your Loveliness and the hour of my death." *Letters,* II, 133. See chapters 7 and 8 for more detailed studies of these twin themes.

[6] Lionel Stevenson has offered an alternative interpretation of these lines. In a note to the author he writes: "I think that 'whose' is correct: Those whom 'eyes can kill' are the enchanters and dragons. She could slay them but she will not do so because she as an 'enchantress,' is on their side. This explains the 'alas': the poet regrets that she is not a force for good. She and the dragons are both opposed to the knight." Regardless of which reading one prefers, the thematic significations are not altered.

eral of the main contentions of this study. Keats's decision to excise the final four lines, for example, may have been based on an awareness of the juvenile flatness of the final couplet, but the first two lines are not so poor and, moreover, they are a distinct aid to an understanding of the poem's theme. Though they are an aid, they are not essential; the submerged relationships in the poem reveal the same thematic significance. True, the theme is not at once available to the reader: it requires considerable elucidation. I think it likely the significance of the images was so lively in Keats's mind that he was unaware that by omitting what would have been lines 69 and 70 his poem would seem less serious.

[2]

Hymning and Harmony

Submerged or fragmented relationships occur in many of Keats's poems, in the well known as frequently as in the little known. Becoming aware of the complexity and coherence of the entire relational system by bringing together for inspection its separate occurrences provides a means of identifying potential and actual significations, and thereby, ultimately, of interpreting both the major and the minor poetry. We shall find that Keats's poems do explain themselves—and each other—though not quite in the way he had in mind (see *Letters,* II, 21).

For example, twice in his early poetry Keats seems to establish a relationship between words that are sounded at the same time and musical harmony. Both times a relationship between words and food is briefly established at the outset. In the sonnet, "How many bards gild the lapses of time!" we are told that the beauties, "earthly and sublime," of a few poets are food that delights the poet's fancy, and that when he sits down to rhyme, these beauties

> will in throngs before my mind intrude:
> But no confusion, no disturbance rude
> Do they occasion; 'tis a pleasing chime.
>
> (lines 6–8)

The sestet says that *in the same manner* four specific kinds of sounds,

The songs of birds—the whisp'ring of the leaves—
The voice of waters—the great bell that heaves
(lines 10–11)

as well as

thousand others more
That distance of recognizance bereaves,
Make pleasing music, and not wild uproar.
(lines 12–14)[1]

Surely there are some senses in which phrases from great
poetry are harmonious: they are, let us say, alike in beauty,

---

[1] The sonnet is heavily indebted to Spenser. As Guyon and the Palmer
approach the bower of bliss,

Eftsoons they heard a most melodious sound,
  Of all that mote delight a daintie eare,
  Such as at once might not on living ground
  Save in this Paradise, be heard elsewhere:
  Right hard it was, for wight, which did it heare,
  To read, what manner musicke that mote bee:
  For all that pleasing is to living eare,
  Was there consorted in one harmonee,
Birdes, voyces, instruments, windes, waters, all agree.

The joyous birdes shrouded in chearefull shade,
  Their notes unto the voyce attempred sweet;
  Th' Angelicall soft trembling voyces made
  To th' instruments divine respondence meet:
  The silver sounding instruments did meet
  With the base murmure of the waters fall:
  The waters fall with difference discreet,
  Now soft, now loud, unto the wind did call:
The gentle warbling wind low answered to all.
                              FQ, II, xii, 70–71.

Both Keats and Spenser emphasize the profusion of voices and the
kinds of voices that combine into harmonious music. Sounds alter in
pitch and volume in both selections. In the sonnet, the bell "heaves
with solemn sound"; in the stanzas from Spenser, the waters are
"Now soft, now loud," and the wind is described as "warbling." Also
stressed is the difficulty of identifying each particular voice in the
several choirs. There can be little doubt that Spenser is one of the
bards who "gild the lapses of time."

elegance, and sincerity. But they would not be harmonious if they were heard simultaneously, for poetry is composed of referential, discursive words. If the "beauties," the phrases, were not composed of recognizable words, if they were bereaved of their meaning rather than their precise locations in their sources, then we would be dealing with poetry as a sort of nonreferential verbal music; there is no evidence that Keats perceived poetry in this way. Even the reference to "Spenserian vowels that elope with ease" in the epistle "To Charles Cowden Clarke" is embedded in a context that emphasizes more referential meanings. Yet both Sidney Colvin and Aileen Ward assume that in the sonnet precise words or phrases are being discussed. Miss Ward suggests that "the echoes of other poets' work that began chiming in his head whenever he started a new poem of his own" were troublesome, a suggestion I think denied by the whole sonnet.[2] Colvin asserts that "the main interest of the sonnet is its comparison of the *working* of Keats's miscellaneous poetic reading in his mind with the *effect* of the confused but harmonious sounds of evening on the ear—a frank and illuminating comment by himself on those stray echoes and reminiscences of the older poets which we catch now and again throughout his work."[3] Amy Lowell is more circumspect; she thinks the sonnet "shows how Keats was haunted by his reading. A fact to which the many 'steals' and forgetful borrowings in all his early work vigorously testifies."[4] We need to realize that most of the poem's commentators assume that the "recognizance" that is missing is conscious recognition and attribution to a precise source of a word or phrase.[5] The relationship then does not imply that lines from

---

[2] Ward, p. 64.

[3] Colvin, pp. 88–89. Emphasis supplied.

[4] Lowell, I, 116.

[5] Pettet too assumes this, though the passage he quotes from Stephen Spender's *World within World* definition of a second type of poetic memory, that which relates another's poetic impulse to one's own, seems to me more relevant. See pp. 7–8 of Pettet's book.

various poems make a pleasing chime when spoken together, but that they are not identifiable. To be sure, four kinds of sound, mostly in the form of voices, are identified in the sestet, but even there we are dealing with imprecise though generically similar sounds: no particular songbird is heard, rather "songs of birds." Similarly, whispering of leaves, voice of waters. What we have are simultaneous chords of similar timbre. Four of these chords blend into a harmony wherein the different timbres are complementary. The relationship between the throngs of beauties and the sounds of nature is far more limited than the "as-so" structure of the sonnet would lead us to believe.

But, as I have stated, there are ways in which lines of poetry are harmonious, do make a pleasing chime. The way Keats may have had in mind can be found in the second poem that seems to establish a relationship between words and harmony, the sonnet "To Kosciusko." In this poem, the absence of such precise significations as we find in "How many bards" allows us to perceive the relationship more readily. Kosciusko's "great name alone / Is a full harvest whence to reap high feeling," that is, the harvest is one of affect, as is, I propose, fancy's food in the earlier poem. Colvin was on the right track with a comparison to "effect." Kosciusko's name is such a harvest because of its association with heroic actions in foreign and domestic battles for liberty and independence. His name is a symbol for his deeds, for the brightest strand in the fabric of his personality, and this symbol contains all the powerful emotional attraction that defenders of freedom always held for Keats. Thus Kosciusko's name is associated in this poem with Alfred's (as it is again in "Sleep and Poetry," lines 387–89) and with "the great of yore." Similarly, I suggest, the bards in their sonnet are in harmony because of the vivid and strongly pleasant feelings produced in the speaker when he thinks of a line of poetry that recalls the total affect of the author's personality.

Kosciusko's name tells the speaker that it, together with other names of heroes, bursts from concealing clouds and becomes part of a harmony. These names, and "Alfred's and the great of yore," these harmonies will commingle and give "tremendous birth / To a loud hymn."[6] Similarly, in "How many bards" harmonious chords eventually combine to "Make pleasing music." I think it is likely that the names chime together because of their bearers' devotion to freedom, an ideal to which Keats was passionately attracted. For example, the "Sonnet on Peace" expresses the wish that Peace will "Let the sweet mountain nymph thy favourite be" (line 8). (This reference to Milton ["L'Allegro," line 36] is not so casual as its obliqueness makes it seem, but fuller discussion must wait.) Again, the poem "Written on 29 May: The Anniversary of the Restoration of Charles the 2nd" urges rejection of tyranny.[7] Keats's attachment to freedom is also seen in "To Hope," where he prays

> Let me not see our country's honour fade:
> O let me see our land retain her soul,
> Her pride, her freedom; and not freedom's shade;
> (lines 32–34)

and in the epistle "To George Felton Mathew," where we learn

---

[6] This idea was popular with Keats early in his poetic career. Compare in "Sleep and Poetry" the discussion of how the imagination used to function in poetry:

> and who could paragon
> The fervid choir that lifted up a noise
> Of harmony, to where it aye will poise
> Its mighty self of convoluting sound
> Huge as a planet.
> (lines 172–76)

And in the same poem we learn of

> the chimes
> Of Friendly voices.
> (lines 350–51)

[7] Garrod, pp. 23–28, cites some of these lines, and some others, as evidence for Keats's Republicanism "strongly tinged with what we call pacifism." p. 24.

> Of those who in the cause of freedom fell;
> Of our own Alfred, of Helvetian Tell;
> (lines 66–67)

and in "Oh how I love," where one of the delights with which he warms his breast is "patriotic lore" (line 9), and where he thinks in the next line of "Milton's fate." Further, according to correspondent "Y" in *The Morning Chronicle* of 27 July 1821, Keats "once said that if he should live a few years, he would go over to South America, and write a poem on Liberty. . . ."[8]

With this supporting evidence, I think it likely that the heroes' devotion to freedom links them in the poem, and I suppose that the hymn will be one of freedom. By limiting the significations of the heroes' names Keats is able to indicate that it is the "high feeling" called forth by them that is similar and, hence, harmonious. Sounds are not dealt with specifically in the sonnet, and the omission of the precise significations that were given in "How many bards" establishes a clear, workable relationship.

In a much later poem, "Lines on Seeing a Lock of Milton's Hair," the personality of the poet is placed in a relationship with the concept of harmony. Milton, hailed as both "Chief of organic numbers" and "Old Scholar of the Spheres," is said to have an unslumbering spirit which "rolls about our ears / For ever and for ever!" (lines 4–5). This spirit, this essence of Milton, as it were, is addressed in the second stanza.

> How heavenward thou soundest,
> Live Temple of sweet noise,
> And Discord unconfoundest
> Giving Delight new joys,
> And Pleasure nobler pinions!
> (lines 11–15)

---

[8] Hampstead ed., VIII, 198.

The speaker pledges that when his emotions are less passionate,[9] when his mind is more philosophical, and when "every childish fashion / Has vanished from my rhyme" (lines 23–24), he will

> Leave to an after-time,
> Hymning and Harmony
> Of thee, and of thy works, and of thy life.
> (lines 26–28)

It seems to me that this poem makes clear that it is Milton's whole spirit that affects the speaker. Milton's life was of a piece, harmonious, and dedicated to freedom, and this life will be praised in a "Hymning and Harmony" that will echo the harmoniousness of the life itself. Once again we can see that a relationship once established in Keats's mind was tenacious, and perhaps it was its feeling of familiarity to him that allowed the relationship to appear in the poetry in what must seem to us fragmented form.

---

[9] Compare *Letters,* II, 209, where Keats writes: "I want to compose without this fever. I hope I one day shall."

Part II:

Consideration of Major Problems

[3]

The Passage of an Angel's Tear

I had become all in a Tremble from not having
written any thing of late.

Letters, I, 133.

The perception of the coexistence and interdependence of grief
and joy is present throughout Keats's poetry, as Professor Perkins notes,[1] and it seems to me that even in the early poetry it
represents far more than a rhetorical "flourish,"[2] though it
rarely forces us to examine its structural relevance. Especially
in three of the minor sonnets, "To one who has been long in
city pent," "Written on a blank space at the end of Chaucer's
tale 'The Floure and the Lefe,'" and "Oh! how I love, on a
fair summer's eve," and in lines 231–38 of "I stood tip-toe,"
the perception is part of a submerged and fragmented relationship that reveals a theory about *catharsis* and the production of
poetry.

"To one who has been long in city pent" tells of the joy the
released prisoner of the city feels upon looking "into the fair /
And open face of heaven" (lines 2–3), and especially

> when, with heart's content,
> Fatigued he sinks into some pleasant lair

---

[1] See, for example, Perkins, pp. 287–88.

[2] *Ibid.*, p. 287.

> Of wavy grass, and reads a debonair
> And gentle tale of love and languishment.
>   (lines 5–8)

After listening to a nightingale and

> Watching the sailing cloudlet's bright career,
>   He mourns that day so soon has glided by:
> E'en like the passage of an angel's tear
>   That falls through the clear ether silently.
>   (lines 11–14)

It is, of course, familiar and clear to Keatsians that tales of "love and languishment" are one of the stimuli of Keats's creative imagination, as is scenery, the "fair paradise of Nature's light" ("I stood tip-toe," line 126), but part of the sonnet is less clear, though equally familiar. The process of life and death, growth and decay, epitomized in the gliding by of the day, is likened to the silent falling of an angel's tear. This relationship seems fairly arbitrary, although the idea of an angel may have developed from the description of another of the speaker's blisses:

> 'Tis very sweet to look into the fair
>   And open face of heaven,—to breathe a prayer
> Full in the smile of the blue firmament.
>   (lines 2–4)

The image of the tear may spring from an association with the speaker's eye, mentioned at the end of line 10 and his mourning in line 12. Still, the simile must seem arbitrary though lovely. This is because it is part of a fragmented relationship, which was probably whole in Keats's mind, but which is only partially expressed in this sonnet. To discover the significance of the line and the relationship it is necessary to examine another sonnet, "Written on a blank space at the end of Chaucer's tale 'The Floure and The Lefe.'"

In this sonnet literature is specifically placed in a relationship with a "little copse" in terms of affect.

> This pleasant tale is like a little copse:
>   The honied lines do freshly interlace
>   To keep the reader in so sweet a place,
> So that he here and there full-hearted stops;
> And oftentimes he feels the dewy drops
>   Come cool and suddenly against his face,
>   And by the wandering melody may trace
> Which way the tender-legged linnet hops.
> (lines 1–8)

Lines 127–40 of "I stood tip-toe" exhibit the same relationship.

> In the calm grandeur of a sober line,
> We see the waving of the mountain pine;
> And when a tale is beautifully staid,
> We feel the safety of a hawthorne glade;
> When it is moving on luxurious wings,
> The soul is lost in pleasant smotherings:
> Fair dewy roses brush against our faces,
> And flowering laurels spring from diamond vases;
> O'er head we see the jasmine and sweet briar,
> And bloomy grapes, laughing from green attire;
> While at our feet, the voice of crystal bubbles
> Charms us at once away from all our troubles:
> So that we feel uplifted from the world,
> Walking upon the white clouds wreath'd and curl'd.

The next line tells us that "So felt he, who first told" the story of Psyche, that is, Apuleius.

The sonnet also tells us that the source of inspiration, the "gentle story," has a "mighty power," one which can relieve the speaker's thirst for glory. He

> Could at this moment be content to lie
>   Meekly upon the grass, as those whose sobbings
>   Were heard of none beside the mornful robbins.
> (lines 12–14)

Again we see sobbing, or tears, associated with the reading of poetry, which produces an affect similar to that produced by certain landscapes.

The burden of the third sonnet, "Oh! how I love," is similar: the "pleasant lair" and "little copse" of the previous sonnets become "A fragrant wild, with Nature's beauty drest" (line 7). In this spot the speaker warms his "breast with patriotic lore" (line 9), and so intensely imagines "Milton's fate" and "Sidney's bier" (line 10) that "their stern forms before my mind arise" (line 11). Or he may

> on wing of Poesy upsoar,
> Full often dropping a delicious tear,
>   When some melodious sorrow spells mine eyes.
>   (lines 12–14)

Now tears are associated more directly with either the creation or the reading of poetry—probably both—and the joy they give is blended with sorrow; yet crying does provide relief: it spells, in the sense of relieves, after spelling, in the sense of enchanting. The cathartic effect of reading poetry is matched, in "I stood tip-toe," by the cathartic effect of creating poetry:

> Young men, and maidens at each other gaz'd
> With hands held back, and motionless, amaz'd
> To see the brightness in each other's eyes;
> And so they stood, fill'd with a sweet surprise,
> Until their tongues were loos'd in poesy.
> Therefore no lover did of anguish die:
> But the soft numbers, in that moment spoken,
> Made silken ties, that never may be broken.
>   (lines 231–38)

Earlier in the same poem we learned:

> He was a Poet, sure a lover too,
> Who stood on Latmus' top, what time there blew

Soft breezes from the myrtle vale below;
And brought in faintness solemn, sweet, and slow
A hymn from Dian's temple; while upswelling,
The incense went to her own starry dwelling.
But though her face was clear as infant's eyes,
Though she stood smiling o'er the sacrifice,
The Poet wept at her so piteous fate,
Wept that such beauty should be desolate:
So in fine wrath some golden sounds he won,
And gave meek Cynthia her Endymion.
                                        (lines 193–204)

Thus there appears to be a relationship in Keats's mind between enjoying nature's luxuries in a certain kind of setting, which has an affect much like that of reading poetry, which makes one cry or think of crying, which is also the result of the poet's sympathetic identification with his subject, which produces a wrought-up state in which poetry is created, thus relieving the anguish of the poetic wrath. Apparently the relational system was so fundamental in Keats's mind that often he could let a part stand for the whole without feeling that a poem was any weaker for the substitution. The "angel's tear" is such a substitution: the speaker in the sonnet experiences cathartic relief—from his physical and emotional imprisonment in the city—as the result of reading a romance in a "pleasant lair / Of wavy grass" (lines 6–7). (The significance of including Philomel, the Nightingale, becomes obvious in the discussion of "The Eve of St. Agnes" that follows.)

Keats's poetry may well have performed for him what we would call "symbolic action." The basic mechanism could have been familiar to Keats because of his friendship with Hazlitt. In 1818 Hazlitt published "On Poetry in General," where, as Meyer Abrams has so succinctly pointed out, Hazlitt "adds the doctrine that it [literature] provides emotional catharsis for its author" to his theory "that at least some literature is a form of *Wunschbild*."[3] Furthermore, "Hazlitt elaborates the concept,

---

[3] Meyer Abrams, *The Mirror and the Lamp* (New York, 1958), p. 142.

which has since become a familiar element in expressive theories, the capacity of art to master, by objectifying, the chaotic press of emotion."[4]

The three sonnets are not the only evidence that Keats held, consciously or unconsciously, such a theory.[5] We are aware as early as the epistle "To my Brother George" of the intensity of Keats's absorption in poetry and his dedication to it despite the thought that as a physician he

---

[4] *Ibid.*, p. 143.

[5] For example, in the Lord Northcliffe Lectures of 1953, Peter Alexander points out the following passage from the letters as an instance of "unconscious elucidation of *catharsis*":

> The excellence of every art is its intensity, capable of making all disagreeables evaporate, from their being in close relationship with Beauty and Truth. Examine *King Lear*, and you will find this exemplified throughout.

"The Greek word Κάθαροις," Professor Alexander continues,

> could be used of purification by fire. The 'disagreeables' that evaporate may be equated with Aristotle's fear and pity. Galen refers to the painful and disquieting elements that are to be expelled as ⌐τά λυπουντα; Keats's 'disagreeables' might serve as a translation of Galen's term." (*Hamlet: Father and Son*, [Oxford, 1955], p. 67.)

Professor Alexander finds that Keats, describing his experience as a reader, "stresses above all else precisely this sense of active mastery required by Professor Trilling. There is no turning aside from the fearful elements of existence; the disagreeables have to be mastered in the intensity of the encounter." (p. 75)

In this connection we ought also to refer to Keats's letter to the George Keatses of 15 April 1819, which contains his remark on the cathartic effect of writing the sonnet, "Why did I laugh?": having written the sonnet, Keats avers that he "enjoyed an uninterrupted sleep—Sane I went to bed and sane I arose" (*Letters*, II, 82). But recall his later remark to the George Keatses that he "is scarcly content to write the best verses for the fever thy leave behind" (*Letters*, II, 209). We can recall as well the September 1818 remark to J. H. Reynolds about "the feverous relief of Poetry" (*Letters*, I, 370).

should be
Happier, and dearer to society.
(lines 111–112)

Immediately he admits this, he begins to describe the kind of happiness he derives from poetry:

At times 'tis true, I've felt relief from pain
When some bright thought has darted through my brain:
Through all that day I've felt a greater pleasure
Than if I'd brought to light a hidden treasure.

The term catharsis was first used in the field of medicine where it refers to purgation; its use in aesthetics is metaphorical. Yet to Keats it would have retained significance in both realms. His choice of Apollo as the presider over his devotion to poetry is hardly accidental, although medicine and poetry are not wed until "The Fall of Hyperion" where the speaker argues:

Sure a poet is a sage,
A humanist, physician to all men.
(lines 189–190)

But far earlier than this we can detect highly medical significations of catharsis in Keats's ideas about poetry. The general or over-all relationship is on this order: an excess of emotion causes the blood to surge and so fill the heart and the blood vessels in the throat that it closes the outlet for words which could, if uttered, provide cathartic relief for the pressure of emotion.

In the lines already quoted from "I stood tip-toe" we found that "no lover did of anguish die" because "their tongues were loos'd in poesy" (lines 236, 235). This phenomenon is presented immediately after Keats's description of the beneficent effects of nature in evening at the time of sunset, when Apollo is in his "Western halls of gold."

> The breezes were ethereal, and pure,
> And crept through half closed lattices to cure
> The languid sick; it cool'd their fever'd sleep,
> And soothed them into slumbers full and deep.
> Soon they awoke clear-eyed: nor burnt with thirsting,
> Nor with hot fingers, nor with temples bursting:
> And springing up, they met the wond'ring sight
> Of their dear friends, nigh foolish with delight;
> Who feel their arms, and breasts, and kiss and stare,
> And on their placid foreheads part the hair.
> Young men, and maidens at each other gaz'd
> With hands held back, and motionless, amaz'd
> To see the brightness in each other's eyes;
> And so they stood, fill'd with a sweet surprise,
> Until their tongues were loos'd in poesy.
> Therefore no lover did of anguish die.
>
> (lines 221–36)

That the sick awake "clear-eyed" and the lovers are specifically described only in terms of the "brightness" of their eyes associates even more closely the healing of the sick and the relieving of anguish by poetry.

We next find this relationship functioning in "Isabella," a poem not composed before February, 1818. In October of 1817 Keats had suffered a severe cold, one which persisted throughout the month and for which, presumably, he took mercury. Given his later susceptibility to sore throats, it is not unlikely that he would have experienced one with this cold too.[6] Whether this is so, and whether it is causal, the physical manifestations of repressed emotion described in the poetry from "Isabella" onward are associated more directly with blood from a full throat and with the throat and voice. Lorenzo vows to "tell my love all plain" (line 38), but cannot.

> So said he one fair morning, and all day
>   His heart beat awfully against his side;

---

[6] In February of 1819 Keats wrote to his sister of "A sore throat which has haunted me at intervals nearly a twelvemonth" (*Letters,* II, 38).

And to his heart he inwardly did pray
    For power to speak; but still the ruddy tide
Stifled his voice, and puls'd resolve away—
    Fever'd his high conceit of such a bride,
Yet brought him to the meekness of a child:
Alas! when passion is both meek and wild!
                              (lines 41–48)

Similarly the imprisoned titans in "Hyperion" are unable to speak because of insufficient oxygen and the anguish this causes their vascular systems.

    Coeus, and Gyges, and Briareüs,
Typhon, and Dolor, and Porphyrion,
With many more, the brawniest in assault,
Were pent in regions of laborious breath;
Dungeon'd in opaque element, to keep
Their clenched teeth still clench'd, and all their limbs
Lock'd up like veins of metal crampt and screw'd;
Without a motion, save of their big hearts
Heaving in pain, and horribly convuls'd
With sanguine feverous boiling gurge of pulse.
                              (Book II, lines 19–29)

In "The Eve of St. Agnes" the syndrome, as I think we may now begin to call it, becomes associated with the Philomela legend. The ritual of St. Agnes' Eve forbids Madeline to speak aloud of the vision she wishes to have:

She clos'd the door, she panted, all akin
To spirits of the air, and visions wide:
No uttered syllable, or, woe betide!
But to her heart, her heart was voluble,
Paining with eloquence her balmy side;
As though a tongueless nightingale should swell
Her throat in vain, and die, heart-stifled, in her dell.
                              (lines 201–207)

Could she have spoken, she might have felt like the nightin-

gale in the ode who "Singest of summer in full-throated ease"
(line 10), which I assume is the condition of the bird in "To
one who has been long in city pent."

This would seem to be the aesthetic and the physical condition to which Keats aspired. The opening stanza of the first
"Ode to Fanny" provides substantiation.

> Physician Nature! let my spirit blood!
>   O ease my heart of verse and let me rest;
> Throw me upon thy Tripod, till the flood
> Of stifling numbers ebbs from my full breast.
> A theme! a theme! great Nature! give a theme;
>   Let me begin my dream.
> I come—I see thee, as thou standest there,
> Beckon me not into the wintry air.
>   (lines 1–8)

Claude Finney suggests some evidence for the date of composition:

> On some night in the early part of February, when he was
> held at home by his sore throat while Miss Brawne was at-
> tending a dance, Keats expressed in an ode the physical
> jealousy which racked him. . . . The verse 'Beckon me not
> into the wintry air,' indicates that he composed the ode be-
> tween February 6 and February 14 when he was confined
> in his room with a sore throat.[7]

After the dance, Keats wrote to Fanny, evidently apolo-
gizing for his expression of jealousy.

> You had a just right to be a little silent to one who speaks
> so plainly to you. You must believe you shall, you will that
> I can do nothing say nothing think nothing of you but what
> has its spring in the Love which has so long been my pleasure
> and torment. On the night I was taken ill when so violent a

---

7 Finney, II, 561–62.

rush of blood came to my Lungs that I felt nearly suffocated—
I assure you I felt it possible I might not survive and of that
moment though[t] of nothing but you.

(Letters, II, 254)

Probably, as Bate suggests,[8] he was bled on that occasion.

As many have pointed out, the composition of the ode was
strongly influenced by Burton's chapters on love melancholy,
and Gittings notes that the poem

. . . begins with a medical metaphor—

> Physician Nature! let my spirit blood!

which is taken straight from Burton, who, on the next page
that Keats read, recommended

> *bloud-letting above the rest* which makes *amantes ne sint
> amentes,* lovers come to themselves, and keep in their
> right mind.

Keats's description of his own unhappy condition is physical
and actual.

> My Temples with hot jealous pulses beat

was his cancelled beginning for stanza II. . . .[9] No matter how
much the stanza owes to Burton and to circumstance, we can
see writ large in it the culmination of the relationship we have
been tracing. The cathartic functions of medicine and poetry
are equated, and the way is prepared for the glorification of
the poet-physician in "The Fall of Hyperion."

---

[8] Bate, p. 637.
[9] Gittings, *Living Year,* p. 194.

[4]
How Well Can the Fancy Cheat?

A more complex system of submerged and fragmented relationships is the one ineluctably bound up with one of the most persistent concerns in Keats's life and poetry: the question of the reality and attainability of the realm of the visionary imagination, which is sometimes asked in terms of the imagination's "proper bound" or in terms of how well the fancy can cheat.

The verb "cheat" bears a burden of dark significations that are too frequently ignored. In the "Ode to a Nightingale" the significations provide an answer to the penultimate and final sets of questions by denying their relevance. If the realm of the visionary imagination is fatally flawed by being forlorn—if it contains no mortals—then because the imagination cannot conceal this fact or trick us into overlooking it, it matters not whether the speaker had a vision or a waking dream, whether he was awake or asleep (and these two sets of questions do not ask the same things). What matters is that whatever answers are given to these questions, the truth already revealed is that man can neither long endure in the realm of the visionary imagination nor can he dupe himself into believing it would be possible or desirable to do so.

Although it may seem awkward to have provided an interpretation of this complex ode at this point and so baldly, it is necessary that my understanding of it be in the reader's mind at the outset of a chapter which constantly refers to the poem as a locus of figurative relationships concerned with the visionary imagination. The other poems relating to the problem are discussed in five separate sections of this chapter because of the varying ways they explain themselves and each other.

If the "Ode to a Nightingale" describes, as many believe, the ultimate failure of the visionary imagination to create, achieve, or maintain an ideal realm where "what we call happiness on earth is repeated in a finer tone," then we need to note that in an early poem, the epistle "To my Brother George," Keats describes what he expects to find in that realm. It is not remarkable to find that Keats was concerned within poetry about poetry in August, 1816, and in May, 1819, for the theme of many of his poems is poetry. But it is remarkable that these two poems should provide such a number of points of similarity in setting, imagery, and the progress of the plot, as well as in counter-theme and feeling.

The epistle begins with a two-and-a-half line description of the physical symptoms the poet has felt when he has thought he would never catch "spherey strains" from the "blue dome," or "hear Apollo's song."

> Full many a dreary hour have I past,
> My brain bewilder'd, and my mind o'ercast
> With heaviness.
>
> (lines 1–3)

In the "Ode to a Nightingale," attainment of the ideal realm takes the speaker away from, allows him to forget, a world

> Where but to think is to be full of sorrow
> And leaden-eyed despairs,
>
> (lines 27–28)

a world where "The dull brain perplexes and retards" escape. Though it is not nearly so explicit in the epistle as in the ode, it is fancy, or imagination, or poesy powered by inspiration's wings that provides the escape that thought cannot.

> There are times, when those that love the bay,
> Fly from all sorrowing far, far away;
> A sudden glow comes on them, naught they see
> In water, earth, or air, but poesy.
>
> (lines 19–22)

The speaker in the ode specifically rejects another way to enter the ideal realm, transportation by intoxication:[1]

> Not charioted by Bacchus and his pards,
> But on the viewless wings of Poesy,
>
> (lines 32–33)

but not before describing the route lushly and lovingly in stanza II. That the pleasures provided by such a "draught of vintage" are not easily forsaken may be discovered in the epistle, where the poet (in his trance) expects to see ladies'

> rich brimm'd goblets, that incessant run
> Like the bright spots that move about the sun;
> And, when upheld, the wine from each bright jar
> Pours with the luster of a falling star.
>
> (lines 39–42)

This sight seems not much different from

> a beaker full of the warm South,
> Full of the true, the blushful Hippocrene,
> With beaded bubbles winking at the brim.
>
> (lines 15–17)

The entranced poet in the epistle is allowed to envision the scene through "enchanted portals opened wide," portals that open

---

[1] Wasserman points out that wine "seemed to promise a sensuous intensity, it is true, but one that, instead of leading to self-annihilation through the projection of self into essence, leads only to a forgetfulness of self. It is, then, a false sort of self-destruction. . . ." p. 189.

When the bright warder blows his trumpet clear,
Whose tones reach naught on earth but Poet's ear.
(lines 31–32)

The voice of the nightingale is not so limited in audibility, for it was heard "In ancient days by emperor and clown" and perhaps by Ruth. Nevertheless it functions as does the warder's trumpet: it is the same song

> That oft-times hath
> Charm'd magic casements, opening on the foam
> Of perilous seas, in faery lands forlorn.
> (lines 68–70)

Stanza v of the "Ode to a Nightingale" begins by postulating that if the poet did lose contact with the physical world the sort of death he *might* experience would be rich and painless, a translation to a finer realm. But in the last line-and-a-half he recognizes that he would in fact

> have ears in vain—
> To thy high requiem become a sod.
> (lines 59–60)

In the epistle another sort of easeful death is anticipated, one in which immortality of the spirit seems to compensate for the death of the body. The poet's "proud eye looks through the film of death," and he murmurs:

> What though I leave this dull and earthy mould,
> Yet shall my spirit lofty converse hold
> With aftertimes.
> (lines 71–73)

The poet then details the sorts of inspirations and delights he will leave to patriots, princes, sages, brides, May queens, and mothers. At that point he will be ready to die: he has had his

visions and left them to his fellow men in poetry. He will leave
the earth by flying—and this mode is important for the comparison—but he does not suggest that he will inhabit an ideal
realm.

> Fair world, adieu!
> Thy dales and hills are fading from my view:
> Swiftly I mount, upon wide spreading pinions,
> Far from the narrow bounds of thy dominions.
> Full joy I feel, while thus I cleave the air,
> That my soft verse will charm thy daughters fair,
> And warm thy sons!
>
> (lines 103–9)

The faery lands in the "Ode to a Nightingale" are "forlorn,"
the realm of the visionary imagination is fatally flawed, and the
poet is brought back to reality by a bell that tolls—a sort of
dying into life. At the same time, the voice of the nightingale
literally flies away, and, with it, the realm of the visionary
imagination which it symbolized. Notice the similarities in diction, and the similarity of the landscape described, in this passage and the one just quoted:

> Adieu! the fancy cannot cheat so well
>   As she is fam'd to do, deceiving elf.
> Adieu! adieu! thy plaintive anthem fades
>   Past the near meadows, over the still stream,
>   Up the hill-side; and now 'tis buried deep
>   In the next valley-glades.
>
> (lines 73–78)

The realm of the imagination, having exerted the full power
of its attractions, is rejected by the speaker in the "Ode to a
Nightingale"; its existence is challenged as being chimerical.
In the epistle the claims of everyday reality are more lightly
dismissed, although the attitude toward death is no less am-

bivalent. Only three-and-a-half lines are devoted to the problem that bulks so large in the later poetry:

> Ah, my dear friend and brother,
> Could I, at once, my mad ambition smother,
> For tasting joys like these, sure I should be
> Happier, and dearer to society.
> (lines 109–12)

Immediately following this passage the poet tells of the delights of "scribbling lines." But it should be noted that the poetry he hoped to write as a result of having seen the realm beyond the enchanted portals included not only "such tales as needs must with amazement spell you" (line 66), but the sort of poetry described as the highest sort in "Sleep and Poetry" and in "The Fall of Hyperion," that which is

> a friend
> To sooth the cares, and lift the thoughts of man.
> ("Sleep and Poetry,")
> (lines 246–47)

The tale the May queen will read to the gay villagers is, typically, a romance, "a tale of hopes and fears" (line 97) of the years he spent in the realm of "Flora, and old Pan" ("Sleep and Poetry," line 102), a country that has as distinctive features of its landscape the musk-rose and the violet, and the month of May, a triad that is part of the plot of ground from which the speaker enters the realm of the imagination in stanza v of the "Ode to a Nightingale."

No doubt the three images just mentioned prove nothing by their appearance in both poems. But taken together with the similarities in setting, the theme of the existence of the realm of the visionary imagination, the counter-theme of the types of death, recurrent diction and metaphors of enchantment and spells, the three images help to show the consistency of the symbolic counters used by Keats in his incessant rethinking and refeeling of his central concerns.

The singing of the nightingale often functions, as we have already noticed, as a signal that entrance into the realm of the visionary imagination is being contemplated or attempted. Another pair of poems will show the familiar relationships at work again, and again we shall find Keats positing alternative endings to the story, solutions to the problems, or attitudes toward the conflict. The epistle "To J. H. Reynolds" is well known as one of Keats's most pessimistic poems, while "Bards of Passion and of Mirth" is an optimistic, lighthearted, but not trivial "rondeau" whose theme is the "double immortality of Poets" (*Letters,* 11, 25).

The nightingale in the so-called "rondeau" not only signals the imminence of penetration beyond heaven's bourne but is an inhabitant of that realm; it not only fulfills a higher function more completely than it does in the "Ode to a Nightingale," but it becomes a symbol of the highest sort of poet and poetry. One of the attractions of the realm of heaven where the souls of poets[2] have half their existence is that it is a realm

> Where the nightingale doth sing
> Not a senseless, tranced thing,
> But divine melodious truth;
> Philosophic numbers smooth;

---

[2] These souls, it is important to note, are like those in the rollicking "Lines on the Mermaid Tavern." They are "Souls of Poets dead and gone," though to an "elysium"—or heaven's bourne—that is yet a tavern. (Apollo is, no doubt, the celestial barkeep.) We have already noticed that wine is frequently mentioned in conjunction with the visionary imagination, though it is not mentioned in "Bards of Passion," unless the nightingale's "senseless, tranced song" refers very obliquely to intoxication. The persistence of the relationship increases the likelihood of this reference.

    Tales and golden histories
    Of heaven and its mysteries.
                (lines 17–22)

Perhaps it is almost too obvious that the song of the nightingale, as Keats describes it in "Bards of Passion," is one in which the beauty-truth identification is complete.

But this poem presents only what might be called a consummation devoutly to be wished. The epistle "To J. H. Reynolds," written some seven months earlier, presents a dark alternative in lines 67–85.

> O that our dreamings all of sleep or wake,
> Would all their colours from the Sunset take:
> From something of material sublime,
> Rather than shadow our own Soul's day-time
> In the dark void of Night. For in the world
> We jostle,—but my flag is not unfurl'd
> On the Admiral staff,—and to philosophize
> I dare not yet! Oh never will the prize,
> High reason, and the lore of good and ill
> Be my award! Things cannot to the will
> Be settled, but they tease us out of thought.[3]
> Or is it that imagination brought
> Beyond its proper bound, yet still confined,
> Lost in a sort of Purgatory blind,
> Cannot refer to any standard law
> Of either earth or heaven?—It is a flaw
> In happiness to see beyond our bourn—
> It forces us in summer skies to mourn:
> It spoils the singing of the nightingale.

Claude Finney perceptively remarks that both the imagina-

---

[3] For discussions of the similarities between elements of this poem and "Ode on a Grecian Urn" see the statements by Pettet and Van Ghent in the appendix and Albert Gérard's article, "Romance and Reality: Continuity and Growth in Keats's View of Art," *K-SJ*, XI (1962), 17–29.

tion and reason fail to "draw soothing thoughts out of suffering." Keats, he says, "could not resolve present evil into ultimate good."[4] The malignant forces of nature were disagreeables that could not be evaporated. Yet specific mention of disagreeables, except for the description of

> Shapes, Shadows, and Remembrances,
> That every other minute vex and please,

which ends 53 lines earlier, does not occur until the paragraph immediately following line 85.[5] The "Enchanted Castle" and its setting which Keats has been describing have all the familiar accouterments we are accustomed to reading about in his descriptions of the realm of the imagination, including enchanted doors and windows, fountains, and a clarion call. Amy Lowell notes that "Keats builds a castle surely, and out of his head (for he has evidently forgotten all but the fact and general impression of Claude's picture)."[6]

It seems to me that the passage in the epistle is a very condensed expression of some familiar concerns, and that it is only a partial expression; it presents only some of the attitudes Keats habitually adopted. First we must notice that it is not philosophy itself that fails, it is Keats's lack of a mind capable of reasoning philosophically. As he has said, "I have never yet been able to perceive how anything can be known for truth by consequitive reasoning—and yet it must be—Can it be that even the greatest Philosopher ever arrived at his goal without putting aside numerous objections?"[7] Nevertheless, Keats valued philosophy: he had intended to "ask Hazlitt in about a years time the best metaphysical road I can take,"[8] and he wrote to Sarah

---

[4] Finney, I, 390.

[5] For examination of the possibility that the lines refer forward, see the following chapter.

[6] Lowell, I, 613.

[7] *Letters*, I, 185.

[8] *Ibid.*, 274.

Jeffrey, "I hope I am a little more of a Philosopher than I was."[9]

If he does not yet possess a philosophic mind, he at least realizes that he cannot will himself into the sort of knowledge he desires, for there are too many disagreeables that cannot easily be dismissed.[10] "High reason, and the lore of good and ill," like the silent form of the philosophic Grecian Urn, "tease us out of thought,"[11] Perhaps, too, the darkening of "our own soul's day-time" is owing to the imagination's inability to free itself totally from its "proper bound." It is not clear why the earth is the location of this "proper bound," unless "proper" looks forward to the conclusion that

> It is a flaw
> In happiness to see beyond our bourn—
> It forces us in summer skies to mourn.[12]

At any rate, the passage seems to argue that the imagination cannot free itself from the earth,[13] cannot enter permanently

---

9 *Ibid.,* II, 116. Compare "God of the Meridian," lines 19–21, where Keats asks to share "the staid philosophy" with Apollo and his "hot lyre."

10 I cannot agree with Bate (despite Bush's concurrence) that what Keats meant by "disagreeables" is "the irrelevant and discordant" (p. 243). Intensity of perception does not consist only of an aesthetic intensity, gusto or instress of inscape. The letter of December 21 argues that West's painting contains unpleasantness whose repulsiveness is not buried by any momentous depth of speculation having been excited. The word speculation argues for a more philosophic interpretation of disagreeables. Not only beauty but truth, or the truthful nature of beauty must be considered in understanding this passage. (See *Letters,* I, 192.)

11 In the second sonnet on fame, only the intemperate, fevered man improperly teases the world for grace and "spoils his salvation for a fierce miscreed" (line 14).

12 See the next section of this chapter for an extended discussion of the notion of "proper bound."

13 As Albert Gérard says, "The perception of the world of romance increases our awareness of the shortcomings of the world in which we live." p. 22.

heaven's bourne, and that it is because this is so that we hear the nightingale's song as a "senseless, tranced thing," a spoiled thing. Were we able to remain in heaven's bourne, as in "Bards of Passion," the song would symbolize the union of beauty, truth, philosophy, imagination, legend and fact:

> divine melodious truth;
> Philosophic numbers smooth;
> Tales and golden histories.

But this fellowship with essence is only attained by the bards after death, a condition rejected in the nightingale ode.

In the light of these two poems, which present in familiar relationships some of Keats's central concerns, we ought to examine Keats's quest as it is defined by Professor Wasserman.

> The ideal condition towards which Keats always strives be-cause it is ideal, is one in which mortal and immortal, dy-namism and stasis, the Dionysian and the Apollonian, beauty and truth, are one. And in the "Ode on a Grecian Urn" and "La Belle Dame Sans Merci" he had traced mortal man's momentary scent to, and his inevitable eviction from, this condition. But if, in his aspirations towards the conditions of heaven's bourne man is unable to draw heaven and earth together into a stable union—and it is part of Keats' scheme of things that he must be unable while he is mortal—then he is torn between the two extremes, grasping after both but at home in neither. . . . If man could confine his aspirations to this physical world, to 'something of material sublime,' he might find a degree of content; but it is of his very nature that, unless he limits himself to the 'level chambers' of mere revelry, he can no more renounce his quest for the ideal than Endymion can renounce his quest for Cynthia.[14]

14 Wasserman, pp. 180–181.

Keats's quest, then, was for the best of both possible worlds.[15] We can all agree with Professor Wasserman that in the major poems Keats's possession of this state was momentary at best, but I think that often we can see that he contemplated what it would be like to enter heaven's bourne before death, as in the epistle to his brother George, or after death, as in "Bards of Passion." That is, I do not find such a well-defined quest for what seems to be quite a complex state in which opposites are reconciled, but rather one which is only a more sophisticated and not much more realistic realm of the visionary imagination. Keats's ideal, as Professor Wasserman defines it, even though it contains opposites, is not much more mature than the simple visionary realm that does not present any choices. I suggest that Keats's maturity lies in his perception and acceptance of irreconcilables, but this was not a comfortable state for the poet. This is easily demonstrated; Keats wrote "Bards of Passion" seven months after the epistle to Reynolds. These comments ought not to be construed as derogatory, for it is the serious playing with possibilities that makes Keats a modern and fully human poet.

> O I have been
> Presumptuous against love, against the sky,
> Against all elements, against the tie
> Of mortals each to each, against the blooms
> Of flowers, rush of rivers, and the tombs
> Of heroes gone! Against his proper glory
> Has my own soul conspired: so my story
> Will I to children utter, and repent.
> There never liv'd a mortal man, who bent
> His appetite beyond his natural sphere,
> But starv'd and died.

---

[15] Jacob D. Wigod also defines Keats's quest in this way: "His ideal, in short, is the best of both worlds, what he can find neither in life nor in art alone." "Keats's Ideal in the 'Ode on a Grecian Urn.'" *PMLA,* LXXII (March, 1957), 117.

. . .
       No, never more
Shall airy voices cheat me to the shore
Of tangled wonder, breathless and aghast.
              ("Endymion," IV, 638–48, 653–55)

As I noted before, it is difficult to determine why earth is the "proper bound" of the imagination. By examining the relationships held in common by the epistle and the "rondeau" we have seen Keats consider the idea that if the mind could entirely free itself from earth and cross heaven's bourne into the realm of the visionary imagination, then happiness might be attained. We have seen too that frequently when Keats was not trying to reconcile the realms of imagination and reality he was postulating what it might be like permanently to achieve the former state. Yet once, in "Lines Written in the Highlands," Keats does detail the horrors of achieving such a quest, of leaving earth forever; another alternative presented itself for consideration.

Commentary on the poem has largely overlooked its relationships with other poems concerning Keats's quest for the realm of the visionary imagination. Amy Lowell writes:

> The first part of the poem is excellent description; just this and no more. Nowhere throughout it do we find the slightest hint of Keats's usual charm when dealing with nature, not once is there a single flash of his genius for evocation. The plod of his feet is echoed in his lines, and we cannot suppress the conviction that the poem was written, not because he could not resist it, but because he wanted to try again to write something about Burns to take the taste of the unsuccessful sonnet out of his mouth. The end is a didactic presentation of the giddiness produced by a contemplation of life's futility in the midst of heroic and rather forbidding scenery.[16]

---

[16] Lowell, II, 62.

To quarrel about the presence or absence of "charm" or flashes of genius may seem trivial in view of Miss Lowell's misreading of the end of the poem. But because life, or reality, is the source of most of the varieties of permanence and stability in the poem, if there is no "charm" it is because of the known horror of being in a state where the charms of nature are unimportant: "the forgotten eye is still fast lidded to the ground" (line 21).

Sidney Colvin does not force the poem to mean something it plainly does not, and so his aesthetic judgments, though brief, are more trustworthy. The lines, he says,

> are written in the long iambic fourteeners of Chapman's *Iliad* . . . perhaps chosen to convey a sense of the sustained continuous trudge of his wayfaring. They are very interesting as an attempt to capture and fix in words certain singular, fluctuating intensities of the poet's mood . . . and afterwards his momentary panic lest the spell of mighty scenery and associations may be too overpowering and drag his soul adrift from its moorings of every-day habit and affection— from the ties of the 'sweet and bitter world'—'of Brother's eyes, of Sister's brow.' In some of the lines expressing these obscure disturbances of the soul there is a deep smouldering fire, but hardly ever that touch of absolute felicity which is the note of Keats's work when he is quite himself.[17]

I think it is worth repeating that Keats's "Journey homeward to habitual self" is not a journey to a personality quite as rigidly structured and indelibly patterned as the last clause of Sir Sidney's comments would have us believe. On the contrary, Keats's perception of alternatives and his willingness to explore them to the core demonstrates his humanity, and accounts, I think, for part of his appeal to the modern world.

Claude Finney finds the "human" in the poem too, but in a different aspect.

---

[17] Colvin, p. 286.

The theme of the poem, representing Keats's reflection upon his excursion into the picturesque parts of England and Scotland, is human rather than romantic.[18] The man, Keats said, who sees places renowned in history and poetry is lifted out of himself, he forgets the cares of life; but after a short reprieve, he is glad to return to the world of human affections. . . .

In this poem, as in his *Hymn to Pan* and his *Epistle to Reynolds,* he recalled the word 'bourn' from Hamlet's soliloquy *To be or not to be.*[19]

Another critic who has examined this poem, again with a different emphasis, is Newell Ford, who finds in it "perhaps the most intimate and striking delineation in all his writings of his perfervid imagination in action."[20] Comparing this with the epistle "To J. H. Reynolds" Ford says,

All that we can be sure of is that "the elevation of the moment" repeatedly carries this poet "beyond the bourn," that in moods of optimism and amid fortunate circumstances he feels he enters into (or envisions) heaven, while in moods of skepticism or amid unfavorable circumstances, he lands in the "Purgatory blind" and wonders whether ecstasy is heaven or idiotism.[21]

---

18 E. C. Pettet suggests that the poem's rejection of self-annulment is unromantic, in one sense, and represents "almost a panic retreat from Romanticism into the ordinary man's comfortable 'normality.'" (p. 287) Perhaps Pettet borrowed the idea of a panic retreat from James R. Caldwell's analysis of the genesis of the poem, in which he amplifies the comment, "It is a very factual poem, focused upon an actual recent event, and full of circumstantial detail; and it gives us a direct representation of a daydream wherein undesired ideas broke violently to the surface. It comprises a train of ideas leading not to an inspired insight of the good and fair, but to a panic apprehension." (Caldwell, p. 38)

19 Finney, II, 422–23.

20 Ford, p. 116.

21 *Ibid.,* p. 117. Compare this account with Murry's: "the intensity of the one condition seems to have been proportioned to the intensity

Wasserman finds that the realization of "man's bond with mankind" is the same realization presented in "La Belle Dame": "No knight-at-arms can remain in the elfin grot because, since he is mortal, he cannot wholly yield himself up to this extra-human realm and gain visionary insight into its nature. He will be impelled to make the visionary physical or will long for 'his friends so long forgot.' "[22]

More is shared by the poems mentioned than a similarity of diction; their central concern is the familiar dilemma posed by the diversity of man's desires, his need to participate in the world and his need to outsoar it. A closer analysis of "Lines Written in the Highlands" will clarify its relationships with other poems on the same theme and will restore to our view a largely ignored facet of Keats's personality. (Neither of the two recent biographies examines this poem.)

The first six lines of "Lines Written in the Highlands" tell of the "charm of footing slow" on terrain "made known by times of old," whether by legend or history, and no matter if "each tale a hundred times be told." The terrain itself is not unpleasant, consisting as it does of plains and heaths. At line seven the speaker begins a description of a "deeper joy," one not surprisingly mingled with pain:

There is a deeper joy than all, more solemn in the heart,
More parching to the tongue than all, of more divine a smart,
When weary steps forget themselves upon a pleasant turf,
Upon hot sand, or flinty road, or sea-shore iron scurf.
(lines 7–10)

The quest over this not necessarily pleasant ground is for

---

of the other. They were polar opposites in the wonderful organism which was John Keats. In the creative indolence his organic continuity with Nature was entire; in the churchyard condition, the discontinuity was entire." (p. 204)

[22] Wasserman, p. 74. Also see Evert, pp. 255–56.

> the castle or the cot, where long ago was born
> One who was great through mortal days, and died of
>   fame unshorn,
>   (lines 11–12)

later specified as "a bard's low cradle-place about the silent North!" (line 28).

One who performs a quest of this sort is indifferent to the landscape which, though possessing some significations of loveliness, also has significations of dreariness and death. We learn that

> Light heather-bells may tremble then, but they are far away;
> Wood-lark may sing from sandy fern,—the Sun may hear his lay;
> Runnels may kiss the grass on shelves and shallows clear,
> But their low voices are not heard, though come on travels drear:
> Blood-red the Sun may set behind black mountain peaks;
> Blue tides may sluice and drench their time in caves and weedy
>   creeks;
> Eagles may seem to sleep wing-wide upon the air;
> Ring-doves may fly convuls'd across to some high cedar'd lair;
> But the forgotten eye is still fast lidded to the ground,
> As Palmer's, that with weariness, mid-desert shrine hath found.
>   (lines 13–22)

The conflicting significations indicate the tension of opposites and the presence of disagreeables that Keats sometimes thinks will be evaporated in the realm of the visionary imagination. Similarly they indicate the more mature perception of the simultaneous presence of joy and grief.

Lines twenty-three and twenty-four present the termination of the quest and the quester's state of being at the completion of the grueling and quasi-religious journey.

> At such a time the soul's a child, in childhood is the brain;
> Forgotten is the worldly heart— alone, it beats in vain.

At line twenty-four, too, begins a description by analogy of the horrible effects of being cut off from the world. It is im-

portant to notice that the escape is complete, the imagination is
not wandering between two worlds where it

> Cannot refer to any standard law
> Of either earth or heaven.
> ("To J. H. Reynolds," lines 81–82)

nor is it, as the epistle stated,

> Beyond its proper bound, yet still confined,
> Lost in a sort of Purgatory blind.
> (lines 79–80)

However, the diction is similar enough to alert us to the nature
of the quest; after all, dead bards spend half their double lives
in the realm of the imagination.

> Aye, if a madman could have leave to pass a healthful day
> To tell his forehead's swoon and faint when first began
>   decay,
> He might make tremble many a one whose spirit had gone
>   forth
> To find a bard's low cradle-place about the silent North!
> Scanty the hour and few the steps beyond the bourn of care,
> Beyond the sweet and bitter world,—beyond it unaware!
> Scanty the hours and few the steps, because a longer stay,
> Would bar return, and make a man forget his mortal way:
> O horrible! to lose the sight of well remember'd face,
> Of Brother's eyes, of Sister's brow—constant to every place;
> Filling the air, as on we move, with portraiture intense;
> More warm than those heroic tints that pain a painter's sense,
> When shapes of old come striding by, and visages of old
> Locks shining black, hair scanty grey, and passions manifold.
> No, no, that horror cannot be, for at the cable's length
> Man feels the gentle anchor pull and gladdens in its
>   strength:—[23]

---

[23] Compare "Endymion," I, 1–11, where, because things of beauty provide bowers and healthful sleep,

One hour, half-idiot, he stands by mossy waterfall,
But in the very next he reads his soul's memorial :—
He reads it on the mountain's height, where chance he may
    sit down
Upon rough marble diadem—that hill's eternal crown.
Yet be his anchor e'er so fast, room is there for a prayer
That man may never lose his mind on mountains black and
    bare;
That he may stray league after league some great birthplace
    to find
And keep his vision clear from speck, his inward sight un-
    blind.

                                                    (lines 25–48)

It is plain that the experience of delaying overlong in the
realm of the visionary imagination is fatal to man's powers of
reason, because the analogue for the experience is provided by
a madman. Despite the fastness of man's anchor in reality, the
need for precaution is not obviated: man might well pray not
to lose his mind while solitarily exploring the mountains of the
imagination. The quest itself is not interdicted, but we are
warned that it is only for the brave, the careful, the mature.
A further gloss on the lines, and to my mind proof of Keats's
modernity, are these lines from Robert Frost's "Birches."

> I'd like to get away from earth awhile
> And then come back to it and begin over.
> May no fate willfully misunderstand me
> And half grant what I wish and snatch me away
> Not to return. Earth's the right place for love:
> I don't know where it's likely to go better.
>   (lines 48–53)

> on every morrow, are we wreathing
> A flowery band to bind us to the earth,
> Spite of despondence, of the inhuman dearth
> Of noble natures, of the gloomy days,
> Of all the unhealthy and o'er-darkened ways
> Made for our searching.
>   (lines 6–11)

The pretty "Song," "I had a dove," was included by Keats in a journal letter to his brother George, 2 January 1819, along with "Bards of Passion" and "Fancy." Despite this proximity, no one has commented on the relationships shared by these three poems. Noticing significations shared by "Fancy" and "I had a dove" will lead to a discovery of the relationships that again lead to the nightingale ode by way of the Highland lines.[24]

"I had a dove" was not published in the 1820 volume, perhaps because Keats intended to work it into a sonnet: this seems to be part of the import of Gittings' comments on the genesis of the poem.

Keats wanted to see his sister again before he left London, and this he did, walking over to Walthamstow on the frosty morning of Monday, December 21st. This may have been the occasion of a poem, for just about this time, Keats wrote the charming song *I had a Dove*. He transcribed it for George shortly afterwards, calling it 'a little thing I wrote off to some Music as it was playing.' Fanny Keats played the piano, and enlivened her dull and restricted life at the Abbeys by keeping livestock, rabbits and pigeons. Keats ended a nonsense poem to her, a few months later [1 May 1819, Rollins thinks], with the lines

> Two or three dove eggs
> To hatch into sonnets—

which might well be a reference to this song.[25]

---

[24] Douglas Bush comments on the "serious note" found in two of three poems. Of "Fancy" he writes: "There runs through the poem a serious note that is to be sounded more deeply in the odes: the sensuous phenomena of nature, tied to natural processes, may perish or cloy as the ideal creations of the roving, unfettered mind do not." Bush remarks that "Bards of Passion" "is a kind of variation on the same theme, the relation and the contrast between transient actuality and ideal permanence." *John Keats: His Life and Writings* (New York, 1966), p. 110.

[25] Gittings, *Living Year*, p. 54.

Amy Lowell thinks that the apparent casualness of the circumstances in which Keats composed the poem "probably accounts for both its subject and its diction."[26] I think Miss Lowell is more right than she knew. Keats's unpremeditated muse produced, I shall show, another poem about fancy and the imagination's proper bound. An explication of the song, which can be thought of as a sonnet lacking the second quatrain, will demonstrate the contention.

> I had a dove and the sweet dove died;
>   And I have thought it died of grieving:
> O, what could it grieve for? it was tied,
>   With a silken thread of my own hand's weaving;
> Sweet little red feet! why did you die—
> Why would you leave me, sweet dove! why?
> You liv'd alone on the forest-tree,
> Why, pretty thing! could you not live with me?
> I kiss'd you oft, and gave you white peas;
> Why not live sweetly, as in the green trees?

The dove, "tied / With a silken thread" seems to be identical to the fancy, which cannot bring pleasure when constrained.[27] The following lines from the poem "Fancy" elaborate on this:

> Ever let the fancy roam,
> Pleasure never is at home:
> At a touch sweet Pleasure melteth,
> Like to bubbles when rain pelteth;
> Then let winged Fancy wander
> Through the thought still spread beyond her:
> Open wide the mind's cage door,
> She'll dart forth and cloudward soar.
> O sweet Fancy! let her loose;
> Summer's joys are spoilt by use.
>
>   (lines 1–10)

---

[26] Lowell, II, 140.

[27] Keats writes in November 1819 of his tethered fancy (*Letters*, II, 234), and in March 1820 that he "will not sing in a cage" (*Letters*, II, 270).

The poem continues by describing how the mind in winter can "Send abroad" (line 25) "Fancy, high-commission'd" (line 27) to bring back "Beauties that the earth hath lost" (line 30) to delight us. In case we missed the point that Fancy brings these back from the realm of the imagination, Keats repeats the message in the last verse paragraph.

> O sweet Fancy! let her loose;
> Everything is spoilt by use;
> Where's the cheek that doth not fade,
> . . .
> At a touch sweet Pleasure melteth
> Like to bubbles when rain pelteth.
> Let, then, winged Fancy find
> Thee a mistress to thy mind:
> . . .
>   Break the mesh
> Of the Fancy's silken leash;
> Quickly break her prison-string
> And such joys as these she'll bring.—
> Let the winged Fancy roam,
> Pleasure never is at home.
>   (lines 67–69, 77–80, 89–94)

Now we have some tools and some information, some shared relationships that we can use to penetrate the charming surface of the song.

With the aid of the verbal parallels, which I am sure are self-evident, we can begin to transfer significations we discover in "Fancy" to the song. It is apparent at once that the dove is a symbol of the fancy, as is so frequently another bird, the nightingale. The fancy perishes when restricted to earth even by the most "gentle anchor" ("Lines Written in the Highlands," line 40). The fancy cannot live with even the most tender master; every mind is a cage, every "silken thread" a "prison string." The mind in winter corresponds to the world; that is, the relationship can be written: the wintery mind is to

the imaginative re-creation of Spring, Summer, and Autumn
as the dove, forced to live in domestic confinement, is to the
free, forest-dwelling bird. "White peas," though elegant, are
not the imagination's proper food: they are as harmful as even
the most gossamer thread. Pleasure is as delicate as a bubble,
and can be destroyed by even a gentle rain, even as white peas
and silken threads destroy the dove. The dove, we can reply,
grieved for its freedom, for the kind of life it enjoyed in its
natural habitat. Though as human beings we might not care or
be able to dwell "alone on the forest tree" (in the realm of the
imagination), away from "Brother's eyes" and "Sister's brow"
("Lines Written in the Highlands," line 40), the fancy cannot
be fully operative when confined to earth, or

> Beyond its proper bound, yet still confined,—
> Lost in a sort of Purgatory blind.
> ("To J. H. Reynolds," lines 78–79)

But the "Song," "I had a dove," like "Bards of Passion" and
the epistle to George, posits the existence of a realm of the
visionary imagination which can be entered and maintained.[28]

There has been a good deal of discussion of the little lyric
"Hush, hush! tread softly," mostly by Murry[29] and Gittings,[30]
and mostly bearing on the legitimacy of biographical infer-

---

[28] Bernice Slote presents an interesting interpretation of the "Song,"
showing how it answers its "probable antecedent, a passage in
Romeo and Juliet (II, ii. 177–184)," but at the same time she demonstrates the inadequacy of her own occasionally autobiographical approach by demolishing only the extreme of that bias: "It is no more
necessary to assume 'Hush, hush!' to be a literal account than to
think that 'I had a Dove' (a charming musical exercise in a child's
voice) proves that Keats had a bird who died in spite of his person-
ally woven silk thread, his kisses, and his gifts of white peas."
pp. 134–35.

[29] The chapter of importance is "Keats and Isabella Jones."

[30] See *Living Year,* the chapter " 'Hush, hush' and Isabella Jones."

ences about Keats's relationship with Mrs. Isabella Jones. One of the major complications is the lack of a verifiable date for the poem. Part of Gittings' argument for 1819 rests on some similarities in "Hush, hush," and "The Eve of St. Agnes." Perhaps the tenacity of relationships once they are established in Keats's mind, a tenacity I have been demonstrating, weakens Mr. Gittings' argument about the date, but it cannot damage the perceptiveness of his comparison.

Hush, hush, in fact, is a miniature rehearsal for the great poem which Keats began to write directly he arrived in Chichester. There are strong likenesses. A cancelled opening to stanza viii of *The Eve of St. Agnes* shows the lines

> She danced along with vague uneager eyes,
> Her anxious lips full pulp'd with rosy thoughts,

which at once recall

> But my Isabel's eyes, and her lips pulp'd with bloom.

In another early stanza of *St. Agnes,* Keats's first draft actually used the exclamation, 'Hush, hush!' itself . . . . Yet it is not trivial to see how it ["The Eve of St. Agnes"] also shares the atmosphere of the little lyric.

> We are dead if the latchet gives one little clink!

anticipates the hero and heroine of the greater poem, stealing at midnight from the sleeping hall. It is not in the least incongruous to think of Isabella's old O'Callaghan as the ancestor of 'that old Lord Maurice' and the other 'hot-blooded lords' whose presence threatens the safety of the lovers in *The Eve of St. Agnes;* for the poem itself was suggested by Isabella.[31]

We have a right to be surprised that Gittings overlooks the

---

[31] Gittings, *Living Year,* p. 60.

parallel between "The old man may sleep" and the Beadsman who "slept among his ashes cold" (line 378).

As interesting as this connection is, there is in "Hush, hush" a submerged relationship with the "Ode to a Nightingale" that is important not biographically but because it sheds light on the fundamental romantic metaphor of organic growth. It is the second and third stanzas of the lyric that are important.

No leaf doth tremble, no ripple is there
   On the river,—all's still, and the night's sleepy eye
Closes up, and forgets all its Lethean care,
   Charm'd to death by the drone of the humming May-fly;
     And the moon, whether prudish or complaisant,
     Has fled to her bower, well knowing I want
No light in the dusk, no torch in the gloom,
But my Isabel's eyes, and her lips pulp'd with bloom.

·Lift the latch! ah gently! ah tenderly—sweet!
   We are dead if that latchet gives one little clink!
Well done—now those lips, and a flowery seat—
   The old man may sleep, and the planets may wink;
     The shut rose shall dream of our loves, and awake
     Full blown, and such warmth for the mornings take,
The stock dove shall hatch her soft brace and shall coo,
While I kiss to the melody, aching all through!

It is commonly accepted that the nightingale ode is a poem concerned with penetration into the realm of the visionary imagination. It is also commonly accepted that metaphors of sexual union are used by Keats to describe the union of opposites—all disagreeables having been melted away—which takes place at heaven's bourne. Examination of the landscape of "Hush, hush" and that of the "Ode to a Nightingale" will demonstrate the existence of this submerged relationship between the two poems.

The lyric describes the stillness of the night:

> No leaf doth tremble, no ripple is there
>   On the river,—all's still,

while in the nightingale ode there is only a hint of a breeze:

> But here there is no light,
> Save what from heaven is with the breezes blown,
>   (lines 38–39)

and at the last we learn of "the still streams" (line 76).
"Hush, hush" further describes the darkness:

> And the moon, whether prudish or complaisant,
> Has fled to her bower, well knowing I want
> No light in the dark, no torch in the gloom.

The lines last quoted from the nightingale ode (38–39) tell us
that the forest is dark even though

> The Queen-Moon is on her throne,
> Cluster'd around by all her starry Fays.
>   (lines 36–37)

In the plot where the bird sings, the speaker "cannot see what
flowers are at my feet" because of the "embalmed darkness"
(lines 41, 43).

The lyric tells us that

> The night's sleepy eye
> Closes up, and forgets all its Lethean care,

much as in the ode the speaker's eye might have been drooping
because of the heartache and "drowsy numbness" he feels, as
though he "Lethe-wards had sunk" (lines 1, 2). But night's
eye is "Charm'd to death by the drone of the humming May-
fly." As the speaker in the nightingale ode thinks synaestheti-
cally of "the murmurous haunt of flies on summer eves" (line
50) he muses:

> Darkling I listen; and, for many a time
> I have been half in love with easeful Death.
>
> (lines 51–52)

It should be noticed that the murmuring flies are associated with May, for one of the sweets guessed by the speaker in the darkness is

> mid-May's eldest child,
> The coming musk-rose.
>
> (lines 48–49)

The musk-rose must be a bud, which is to say, a rose like the one described in the lyric:

> The shut rose shall dream of our loves, and awake
> Full blown.[32]
>
> (lines 21–22)

In their "flowery seat," which can be considered as an abstract description of the particularized flora in the fifth stanza of the nightingale ode, the lovers in the lyric will "Kiss to the melody, aching all through!" Similarly, in the ode, the speaker's heart aches while listening to the song of the nightingale emanating from a "melodious plot" (line 8).

Thus the realm of the visionary imagination, the goal of the poet's efforts, is described in much the same language as the trysting place of the lovers. The relationship between sexual union and the poetic union of opposites in heaven's bourne (most familiar in "Endymion") is seen to occur in the same environment, and the fragmented relationship between poetic creation and sexual creation can be detected by paying attention to the significations included in the description of landscape in the two poems.

---

[32] Compare "The Eve of St. Agnes," line 36: "Sudden a thought came like a full-blown rose."

How well, then, can the fancy cheat? Sometimes very well indeed; at other times, scarcely well enough. It is as important to be aware of Keats's changing answers as it is to be able to answer the question for each poem that propounds it—no matter how obscure the method of presentation. Once we recognize his incessant questioning and his changing answers we will be more aware of the painful conflicts experienced by the man and more aware of how the whole canon is interrelated and interdependent in structure and texture. We will be less prone to generalize about Keats's thought and more sensitive to his thoughts. We may demote him in the hierarchy of philosophers, but at the same time we shall elevate him in the state of poets.

[5]

Shapes, Shadows, and Remembrances

As we have already seen, Keats's epistle "To J. H. Reynolds" exhibits relationships held in common with several other poems dealing with the realm of the imagination where all disagreeables are evaporated. There is yet another poem that needs to be brought into the discussion because of its relationship to the epistle. The sonnet "To Sleep" will prove again that the problem of disagreeables was never really solved.[1]

Before examining the relationship let us look first at some of the lines from the epistle and then at DeSelincourt's comments on their theme.

> Still do I that most fierce destruction see,
> The Shark at savage prey—the Hawk at pounce,
> The gentle Robin, like a Pard or Ounce,
> Ravening a worm—Away ye horrid moods,
> Moods of one's mind!
>
> (lines 102–6)

DeSelincourt observes:

> Keats returns to the problem of Nature's cruelty in a letter written a year later, and shows himself far more able to grapple with it. ". . . I perceive how far I am from any humble

[1] See Albert Gérard's article "Romance and Reality: Continuity and Growth in Keats's View of Art," *K-SJ*, XI (1962), for the argument that the "Ode on a Grecian Urn" presents the evaporation.

standard of disinterestedness. Yet this feeling ought to be carried to its highest pitch, as there is no fear of its ever injuring society—which it would do, I fear, pushed to an extremity. For in wild Nature the Hawk would loose his Breakfast of Robins and the Robin his of worms—the Lion must starve as well as the Swallow. The greater part of Men make their way with the same instinctiveness, the same unwandering eye from their purposes, the same animal eagerness as the Hawk. The Hawk wants a mate, so does the Man—look at them both, they set about it and procure one in the same manner. . . . The noble animal Man for his amusement smokes his pipe—the Hawk balances about the clouds—that is the only difference of their leisures. This it is that makes the Amusement of Life—to a speculative Mind— I go among the fields and catch a glimpse of a Stoat or a fieldmouse peeping out of the withered grass—the creature hath a purpose, and its eyes are bright with it. I go amongst the buildings of a city and I see a man hurrying along— to what? The creature has a purpose and his eyes are bright with it. But then, as Wordsworth says, 'we have all one human heart—'. There is an electric fire in human nature tending to purify—so that among these creatures there is continually some birth of new heroism. The pity is, that we must wonder at it, as we should at finding a pearl in rubbish."[2]

Scarcely a month later (21 April 1819), in the same journal letter to George and his wife, we find Keats still seemingly confident in this understanding of Nature's cruelty. In the famous "Vale of Soul-making" passage he writes: "Do you not see how necessary a World of Pains and troubles is to school an Intelligence and make it a soul? A Place where the heart must feel and suffer in a thousand diverse ways!"[3]

---

[2] DeSelincourt, p. 539.

[3] *Letters*, II, 102. Earlier comments on the same theme include these three. First, in the letter to Bailey of 22 November 1817 Keats writes: "The first thing that strikes me on hea[r]ing a Misfortune having befalled another is this. 'Well it cannot be helped.—he will have the pleasure of trying the resources of his spirit. . . ." (*Letters*, I, 186).

Nine days later Keats copied into the same letter the sonnet
"To Sleep."

> O soft embalmer of the still midnight,
>   Shutting, with careful fingers and benign,
> Our gloom-pleas'd eyes, embower'd from the light,
>   Enshaded in forgetfulness divine;
> O soothest Sleep! if so it please thee, close
>   In midst of this thine hymn, my willing eyes,
> Or wait the amen, ere thy poppy throws
>   Around my bed its lulling charities;
>   Then save me, or the passed day will shine
> Upon my pillow, breeding many woes;
>   Save me from curious conscience, that still hoards
> Its strength for darkness, burrowing like a mole;
>   Turn the key deftly in the oiled wards,
> And seal the hushed casket of my soul.

The difficult lines (10 and 11) are explained by Miss Lowell as

> really as plain as day. Any one who has suffered from in-
> somnia will attest their absolute truth, for who, lying
> awake at night, has not found the events of the day before
> full of thorns to prick his sensitive midnight consciousness
> withal?[4]

The sonnet is reminiscent too of the analogy for the "atom
darkness in slow turmoil," in "Isabella," (line 322) where we
learn of Isabella's experiences after her dream of the murdered
Lorenzo:

> As when of healthful midnight sleep bereft
>   Thinking on rugged hours and fruitless toil,

Second, in the letter to Reynolds written the same day, "Why don't
you, as I do, look unconcerned at what may be called more particularly
Heart-vexations? They never surprize me—lord! a man should have
the fine point of his soul taken off to become fit for this world,"
(*Letters*, I, 188). Third, see the whole letter to Reynolds of 3 May
1818, on the Chambers of Life idea.

[4] Lowell, II, 236.

    We put our eyes into a pillowy cleft,
      And see the spangly gloom froth up and boil.
                        (lines 323–26)

I have a strong suspicion that Keats's insomnia was caused in part by thoughts of nature's cruelty.[5] The mysterious tale of a quiet eve that so upset Keats produced insomnia and fantastic visions. To be sure, as I suggested, the tale poisoned Keats's faith in the realm of the imagination, but, as we saw, it began by disrupting his sleep as well. The epistle begins:

    Dear Reynolds! As last night I lay in bed,
    There came before my eyes that wonted thread
    Of Shapes, and Shadows, and Remembrances,
    That every other minute vex and please:
    Things all disjointed come from north and south,—
    Two Witch's eyes above a Cherub's mouth,
    Voltaire with casque and shield and habergeon,
    And Alexander with his nightcap on;
    Old Socrates a-tying his cravat,
    And Hazlitt playing with Miss Edgeworth's cat;
    And Junius Brutus, pretty well so, so,
    Making the best of's way towards Soho.
    Few are there who escape these visitings,—
    Perhaps one or two whose lives have patent wings,
    And through whose curtains peeps no hellish nose,
    No wild-boar tushes, and no Mermaid's toes.
                     (lines 1–16)

Despite the playful tone, the experience was painful. Keats refers back to it at line sixty-seven:

    O that our dreamings all, of sleep or wake,
    Would all their colours from the sunset take:
    From something of material sublime,

---

[5] As opposed to bad dreams associated with a picture of a Methodist meeting. See *Letters,* II, 260, 271, 277.

> Rather than shadow our own soul's day-time
> In the dark void of night.
>
> (lines 67–71)

I am suggesting that it is not altogether appropriate to interpret the sonnet by thinking merely of the general condition of insomnia or by attributing to Keats a tender ethical conscience. But even if Miss Lowell's reading is more accurate than I believe, it is so only for lines eleven and twelve, not lines nine and ten. There is no firm indication that the things the speaker asks to be saved from are identical. The passed day shining on his pillow is figuratively equivalent to the shadowing of the "soul's day time / In the dark void of night," and it is not necessarily the same as curious conscience.[6]

It is not difficult to see that the painful experiences of his soul in the daytime, or more precisely, during the quiet eve when he

> Saw too distinct into the core
> Of an eternal fierce destruction
>
> (lines 96–97)

were the substance of his dreams, and that the experience bred its woes on his pillow. As in Plato's cave, reality was shadowed forth, not presented directly; it was converted into the distorted dream described in the opening section. Perhaps Keats was unable to sleep that night in April, 1819, because he was not yet able to accept emotionally his ideas about the educational values of nature's cruelty.

---

[6] Why conscience should be "curious" at all is something of a problem. If "curious" means strange rather than "inquisitive," conscience may be strange because it works in the dark and, hence, man is unable to form an accurate picture of it. But if "curious" means inquisitive, then "conscience" probably refers to the mind that makes ethical judgments. The latter reading makes identical the two things from which the speaker asks to be saved, but they would be identical in such a way that my interpretation, not Miss Lowell's would be supported.

[6]

The Ache of Ignorance

I find that I can have no enjoyment in the World but continual drinking of knowledge.

(Letters, I, 271)

Every department of knowledge we see excellent and calculated toward a great whole. . . . An extensive knowledge is needful to thinking people—it takes away the heat and fever.

(Letters, I, 277)

Five sonnets deal with the problem of the "agony of ignorance," as Keats phrased it in the famous journal letter of February to May, 1819, which contains two of the poems: "Why did I laugh to-night?" and "How fever'd is the man?" The letter is the *locus classicus* for discussion of Keats's achieving the philosophy of disinterestedness, of his recognition that disagreeables must be part of life. I have already discussed one stage of this philosophic quest for acceptance in my examination of another sonnet appearing in the letter, "To Sleep." Continuing to trace chronologically the problem of ignorance and Keats's attitudes toward it will allow us to see Keats positing several solutions, none of which wholly satisfied him, for each was succeeded by another. Death seems to be the solution posed most frequently in poems of the time, as for example in "Ode to a Nightingale,"[1] "To Sleep," and "Hyperion."[2]

The earliest sonnet of the five, "To the Nile," argues that recognition of our own lack of first-hand experience or information frustrates us and, unless we are careful, prevents us from questioning intelligently and from trusting the normal human process of thinking, especially of thinking by analogy. In the sonnet Keats is also suspicious of second-hand knowledge, but finally he is able to dismiss his dark fancies by extending his knowledge of English nature to Egypt. (Ironically, the extension is incorrect; as Amy Lowell put it, "There are 'no green rushes like our rivers' in the Nile, but Keats can conceive of no river without them. The Nile in his hands, through

---

[1] As DeSelincourt observes of the line "Yet would I on this very midnight cease," in "Why did I laugh to-night?": "All critics have called attention to the repetition of the idea and language of this line in the *Ode to the Nightingale* [sic] composed within the next two months. 'To cease upon the midnight with no pain'." (p. 549) In this chapter and the next I am concerned with the manifold relationships "Why did I laugh to-night?" shares with other poems. Douglas Bush notes briefly that the "rather rhetorical sonnet is not an isolated utterance" and suggests links with the letters, *Hyperion,* the sonnet written on top of Ben Nevis, "When I have fears," and the "Ode to a Nightingale." (Bush, p. 122)

[2] In "Hyperion," III, 61-end, as Gittings points out, "The speech of Apollo himself is full of echoes of Keats's own mood and manner in this crisis. There are the same rhetorical questions, the same reiteration of 'dark, dark'—'darkness, darkness'—and the mental state is exactly repeated, 'with no Agony but that of ignorance'—

In fearless yet in aching ignorance.

The agonies which fill Apollo's brain

As if some blithe wine,
Or bright elixir peerless I had drunk,

are the agony which filled Keats's mind and which produced the philosophy of the letter and the sonnet." *Living Year,* 100–101. Neither Gittings nor Finney, who discusses the sonnet "Why did I laugh to-night?" and "Hyperion" in II, 533–34, discovers the progressive changes in Keats's attitudes toward the likelihood or the difficulties of gaining this knowledge.

courtesy and compliment, turns into an English stream."[3])

> Son of the old moon-mountains African!
>   Stream of the Pyramid and Crocodile!
>   We call thee fruitful, and, that very while
> A desert fills our seeing's inward span.
> Nurse of swart nations since the world began,
>   Art thou so fruitful? or dost thou beguile
>   Such men to honour thee, who, worn with toil,
> Rest them a space 'twixt Cairo and Decan?
> O may dark fancies err! they surely do;
>   'Tis ignorance that makes a barren waste
> Of all beyond itself. Thou dost bedew
>   Green rushes like our rivers, and dost taste
>   The pleasant sun-rise. Green isles hast thou too,
>   And to the sea as happily dost haste.

The relationship between organic evolution and the acquisition of knowledge, and especially Keats's use of the cycle of day and night as equivalents for knowledge, can be found in the unrhymed sonnet to Reynolds, commonly titled, "What the Thrush Said."

> O thou whose face hath felt the Winter's wind,
>   Whose eye has seen the snow-clouds hung in mist,
>   And the black elm tops 'mong the freezing stars,
>   To thee the spring will be a harvest time.
> O thou whose only book has been the light
>   Of supreme darkness which thou feddest on
>   Night after night, when Phoebus was away,
>   To thee the Spring shall be a triple morn.
> O fret not after knowledge—I have none,
>   And yet my song comes native with the warmth.
> O fret not after knowledge—I have none,
>   And yet the evening listens. He who saddens
>   At thought of idleness cannot be idle,
>   And he's awake who thinks himself asleep.

---

[3] Lowell, I, 571.

The sonnet "To Homer," is even more optimistic about the evolution of knowledge than the unrhymed one: the expense of pain in the quest for knowledge is ignored, but it reappears later, with tremendous intensity, in "Hyperion."

> Standing aloof in giant ignorance,
>   Of thee I hear and of the Cyclades,
> As one who sits ashore and longs perchance
>   To visit dolphin-coral in deep seas.
> So thou wast blind!—but then the veil was rent;
>   For Jove uncurtain'd Heaven to let thee live,
> And Neptune made for thee a spumy tent,
>   And Pan made sing for thee his forest-hive;
> Aye, on the shores of darkness there is light,
>   And precipices show untrodden green;
> There is a budding morrow in midnight,—
>   There is a triple sight in blindness keen;
> Such seeing hadst thou, as it once befel
>   To Dian, Queen of Earth, and Heaven, and Hell.

The first lines may be periphrastically rephrased: like one who is longing to breathe the pure serene of knowledge, I stand removed by my ignorance, and take hope from your story, Homer. Since Homer's blindness, his darkness, his ignorance, were mitigated, Keats thinks his might be too.

Bate comments on the similarity in thought between this sonnet and the earlier "What the Thrush Said" without remarking that the same relationship is at work in both sonnets. He quotes lines nine, ten, and eleven of "To Homer" and writes: "This had been the thought of the fine, gently brooding poem 'What the Thrush Said': the answer to come would be tentative . . . but the understanding would still come, gradually, and with all the more 'native' a fulfillment."[4] Aileen Ward relates the sonnet to Reynolds with the one "To Spenser," in regard to the creation of poetry, and though her analysis is perceptive, she overlooks the place of "What the Thrush Said"

---

[4] Bate, p. 641.

in the group of poems I am discussing and its relationship with "Specimen of an Induction," which I discuss in the tenth chapter. Miss Ward writes:

Keats was beginning to recognize in himself a rhythm of energy and indolence, of alternation between the masculine imposition of self upon experience and the feminine surrender to it.[5] This indolence could be a delight, as when he gave himself up to the beauty of an early spring morning; at other times it took the form of a paralysing blankness of feeling and thought, as in the autumn before, when he had wondered whether there was something "radically wrong" with his nature. But now he was beginning to accept these swings of mood, as he did his shifts of philosophical position, as not only inevitable but fruitful in the end. A few weeks later he was to develop this idea in one of his most characteristic metaphors, in a sonnet on "The Human Seasons." Recognizing this fact of his nature, he could now wait more patiently for the "very gradual ripening" of intellect which he realized would be necessary for *Hyperion*—a longer period of "sucking the Sap from mould ethereal." A year or two earlier, he had described the writing of poetry in terms of a journey, a battle, a cliff to be scaled, a vast sea to be explored: now he saw it in images of grain ripening, of wine ageing, of the sun rising and setting, of the flower which

> must drink the nature of the soil
> Before it can put forth its blossoming.

As he wrote to Taylor at this time, 'If Poetry comes not as

---

[5] Fausset writes, "That Keats's sensibility had responded at first by choice to luxurious and fanciful art is significant of his temperament, which was passively receptive to an unusual degree. We can trace this tendency to languor and sloth through most of his poetry; it is evident, as a recent writer has noticed, in his love of stillness, and even more apparent in the worst vices of his style. . . . But it was only a virtue uncontrolled, the feminine quality of receptivity for a time more powerfully resident in him than that male quality of assertion, which inevitably increased with the growth of his mind." (pp. 17–18)

naturally as leaves to a tree it had better not come at all.' [6]

We shall see, however, that Keats's acceptance of the slow process of growth and maturation was not complete.[7] Even the last lines of the letter in which the poem is included tell us of Keats's anxiety about knowledge, but discussion of this must be deferred momentarily so that I can introduce Claude Finney's explicit interpretation of the Wordsworthian influence on Keats's ideas of the growth of knowledge. Finney argues,

> He was inclined, in this mood of mental exhaustion, to accept Wordsworth's philosophy of natural education, according to which sensations or sensuous impressions, which are the primary sources of knowledge, inform man's mind, impress it with quietness and beauty, and feed it with lofty thoughts. These sensations, according to empirical philosophy, develop into complex ideas by means of the process of association. Keats derived the principle of 'wise passiveness,' it is probable, from Wordsworth's *Expostulation and Reply* and *Tables Turned.* . . .
> [In "The Tables Turned"] Wordsworth's natural preachers, the linnet and the throstle, correspond to Keats's thrush, who sings a song of 'wise passiveness.'[8]

Keats, being a clear thinker, knew that the song of his thrush was only partly true; and after he had copied the sonnet for Reynolds he observed:

> Now I am sensible that all this is mere sophistication, however it may neighbor to any truths, to excuse my own indolence. . . .

---

[6] Ward, pp. 166—67.

[7] See too the earlier letter to George and Tom, 23 January 1818: "I think a little change has taken place in my intellect lately–I cannot bear to be uninterested or unemployed, I, who for so long a time, have been adicted to passiveness–nothing is finer for the purposes of great productions than a very gradual ripening of the intellectual powers." (*Letters*, I, 214)

[8] Finney, I, 367–68.

And, writing to his brothers on 21 February 1818, he recalled his previous mood ironically:

> I am reading Voltaire and Gibbon, although I wrote to Reynolds the other day to prove reading of no use. . . .[9]

These last quotations from Keats's letters are vital, for they show that Keats continues to torment himself about idleness. Whether or not his musings on the salutary effects of indolence and associationism are true, he felt guilty about indulging such moods, about not being, if not a philosopher, at least more philosophic.

The next link in this chain of attitudes is the magical and painful transformation of Apollo from thoughtless youth to god. Apollo says:

> For me, dark, dark,
> And painful vile oblivion *seals my eyes:*
> I strive to search wherefore I am so sad,
> Until a melancholy numbs my limbs;
> And then upon the grass I sit, and moan,
> Like one who once had wings.—O why should I
> Feel curs'd and thwarted, when the liegeless air
> Yields to my step aspirant?
> . . . .
>   Where is power?
> Whose hand, whose essence, what divinity
> Makes this alarum in the elements,
> While I here idle listen *on the shores*
> In fearless yet in aching ignorance?
> O tell me, lonely Goddess, by thy harp,
> That waileth every morn and eventide,
> Tell me why thus I rave, about these groves!
> Mute thou remainest—mute! yet I can read
> A wondrous lesson in thy silent face:
> Knowledge enormous makes a God of me.

---

[9] *Letters,* I, 237

Names, deeds, grey legends, dire events, rebellions,
Majesties, sovran voices, agonies,
Creations and destroyings, all at once
Pour into the wide hollows of my brain,
And deify me, as if some blithe wine
Or bright elixir peerless I had drunk,
And so become immortal.
. . . .
Soon wild commotions shook him, and made flush
All the immortal fairness of his limbs;
Most like the struggle at the gate of death;
Or liker still to one who should take leave
Of pale immortal death, and with a pang,
As hot as death's is chill, with fierce convulse
Die into life.

> ("Hyperion," III, 86–93, 103–20,
> 124–30; italics added)

The agony of obtaining knowledge is likened to a struggle with death in which death is defeated. It is important to notice that ignorance and the acquisition of knowledge are painful, though tasting the Pierian spring is not unpleasant at first, when it is apparently spiked with alcohol.

Even the possession of knowledge is no guarantee against agony, for some knowledge is painful while some is not a sufficient anodyne against the disagreeables present in life. The sonnet "Why did I laugh to-night?" is the darkest of the group of poems we have been examining.[10]

Why did I laugh to-night? No voice will tell:
    No God, no Demon of severe response,
Deigns to reply from Heaven or from Hell.
    Then to my human heart I turn at once.

---

[10] Miss Slote admits her violation of chronology in her analysis of the problems of "black brightness" and the sonnet, "Why did I laugh to-night?" Nevertheless she underemphasizes the later changes in his attitudes to show the budding of what she considers a mature perception of opposites. (p. 40)

Heart! Thou and I are here sad and alone;
　　Say, wherefore did I laugh? O mortal pain!
O Darkness! Darkness! ever must I moan,
　　To question Heaven and Hell and Heart in vain.
Why did I laugh? I know this Being's lease,
　　My fancy to its utmost blisses spreads;
Yet I would on this very midnight cease,
　　And the world's gaudy ensigns see in shreds;
Verse, Fame, and Beauty are intense indeed,
But death intenser—Death is Life's high meed.

No god will provide the knowledge Keats asks for, as one
did for Apollo; no heart will be granted "triple vision" as was
Homer's:

Such seeing hadst thou, as it once befel
To Dian, Queen of Earth, and Heaven, and Hell,

but the speaker in this sonnet does have some knowledge:

I know this Being's lease,
My fancy to its utmost blisses spreads.

Despite these consolations, he is willing, if not eager, to die a
rich death. To understand the sort of knowledge he has, we
must look at yet another sonnet, "How fever'd is the man?"

'You cannot eat your cake and have it too'—Proverb

How fever'd is the man, who cannot look
　　Upon his mortal days with temperate blood,
Who vexes all the leaves of his life's book,
　　And robs his fair name of its maidenhood;
It is as if the rose should pluck herself,
　　Or the ripe plum finger its misty bloom,
As if a naiad, like a meddling elf,
　　Should darken her pure grot with muddy gloom;

But the rose leaves herself upon the briar,
  For winds to kiss and grateful bees to feed,
And the ripe plum still wears its dim attire,
  The undisturbed lake has crystal space;
  Why then should man, teasing the world for grace,
Spoil his salvation for a fierce miscreed?

Here we learn again of what Keats used to call his "store /
Of luxuries" ("Sleep and Poetry," lines 346–47), of the things
that belong in his "world of blisses" ("I stood tip-toe," line 54).
The natural world, correctly and disinterestedly observed,[11]
speaks of salvation for man in his perception of the immutable
laws of process, and questioning seems nearly blasphemous. A
man who continues to torment his existence in this way is
fevered, he is unwell, as is, I suggest, the speaker in "Why
did I laugh to-night?", who is so anguished by his ignorance
and his knowledge that his excess emotion spills over in quasi-
hysterical laughter.

The solution suggested in the second sonnet on fame is
preceded by a proverb, and it is pretty to think that the comfort
and sanity Keats wrote of in the journal letter before copying
"Why did I laugh to-night?" were achieved through the
catharsis provided by writing the sonnet and because his life
illustrated the proverb.

Nothing ever becomes real till it is experienced— Even a
Proverb is no proverb to you till your Life has illustrated
it—[12] I am ever affraid that your anxiety for me will lead
you to fear for the violence of my temperament continually

---

11 John L. Mahoney discusses the metaphor of fame and the "false conception" of the "busy pursuit of the fickle woman," contrasting this
with "the true concepeion[sic], that of selfless devotion to the cause
of beauty" which "is seen through images of passivity." *English
Studies,* XLIV (October 1963), 357. ["Keats and the Metaphor of
Fame."]

12 Compare the letter to Reynolds of 3 May 1818, where Keats writes,
"for axioms in philosophy are not axioms until they are proved upon
our pulses." (*Letters* I, 279) Again, in the letter to the George Keatses

smothered down: for that reason I did not intend to have
sent you the following sonnet—but look over the last two
pages and ask yourselves whether I have not that in me
which will well bear the buffets of the world. It will be the
best comment on my sonnet; it will show you that it was
written with no Agony but that of ignorance; with no thirst
of any thing but knowledge when pushed to the point though
the first steps to it were throug[h] my human passions—they
went away, and I wrote with my Mind—and perhaps I must
confess a little bit of my heart. . . . I went to bed, and enjoyed an uninterrupted sleep—Sane I went to bed and sane
I arose.[13]

Occurring as it does in a letter containing the heart of Keats's
mature philosophical speculation, the second sonnet on fame
does not reflect a refusal to question, but rather the result,
however temporary, of experiencing the truth of the proverb.

The expressive functioning of the figurative relationships in
"How fever'd is the man?" was far from completely analyzed
in the preceding section of this chapter. The submerged dia-
lectic of the poem established by the figurative relationships in
which the ideas are conveyed compares a man who torments
his existence for answers to momentous questions of ignorance,
knowledge, and earthly fame as seen in Christian perspective to
a man who masturbates; the man able to accept traditional
religious teaching is chaste, even saintly.

Significations of religion are obvious in "grace," "salvation,"
"miscreed," and they are intensified by the iteration of "mortal
days" and "the leaves of his life's book." Opposed to the calm
and silence of religious wisdom is the fever of autoerotism.
The octave describes the man who vexes himself as the usurper

of 31 December 1818, he writes, "I have made up my Mind never to
take anything for granted—but even to examine the truth of the
commonest proverbs." (*Letters*, II, 18)

[13] *Letters*, II, 81–82.

of his maidenhood—his chastity. He is likened to a rose that plucks itself and a plum that fingers itself; both relationships bear sexual significations too obvious to mention were it not that they are scarcely ever mentioned. An allied sexual experience is pollution, unconscious masturbation that in the case of males includes emission of semen at other times than in coition.

Such would seem to be one of the meanings of lines seven and eight in which the naiad, a female spirit, is likened to an elf, which may of course be male, who by "meddling" darkens "her pure grot with muddy gloom." The lines contain much more literal suggestions of pollution than appear at first glance.

The sestet also employs the rose, the plum, and water—the lake—to convey figuratively the emotional temperateness of calm acceptance of traditional religious wisdom and consolation. The rose no longer plucks itself but

> leaves herself upon the briar
> For winds to kiss and grateful bees to feed.
>   (lines 9–10)

The meaning is complex. The briar may be seen as protection for the rose's chastity. The second part of the relationship suggests proper heterosexual creative processes. I suggest that both chastity and heterosexual creativity are posited as Christian alternatives to autoerotism. The significations of both parts of the lines overlap in presenting acceptable, traditional modes of acceptance and behavior.

The plum's "dim attire" is not designed to be sexually attractive; it suggests nuns' habits or monks' robes. As in the case of the rose, there is considerable tension between conflicting significations: the inner sensuousness of the "ripe plum" is concealed by its outer garb of "misty bloom."

Figurative relationships exhibiting conflict between certain religious attitudes and sexuality are not surprising in view of traditional Christianity's opposition to sexuality, especially autoerotism. Wilhelm Stekel quotes Romans 8.6: "For to be carnally

minded is death; but to be spiritually minded is life and peace,"
and comments:

> That phrase contains the gist of the opposition of religion to
> sexuality. It would be meaningless if we did not know that
> death means loss of salvation, while under 'life and joy' we
> are to understand compensation in the other life. With ad-
> mirable persistence the church has always insisted on the
> sacrifice of sexual pleasure as the price of eternal bliss.[14]

Stekel also describes how ethical considerations magnify more
secular fears, including indolence.

> The masturbator experiences his most serious conflict when-
> ever religious inhibitions are linked to the others. The fear
> inspired by the written and oral teachings that the habit ruins
> health, that it brings on spinal cord trouble, impotence, and
> early invalidism, or that it destroys one's mental energies is
> strengthened by this ethical emphasis. The masturbator feels
> himself in the throes of a vice, he thinks that he has not the
> right to consider himself a 'pure man' and that he commits
> sin. His religious inhibitions render the struggle more signifi-
> cant, more bitter and difficult. It is not merely a question of
> earthly welfare, one's hope of salvation is at stake. Thus in
> fighting the habit the masturbator fights also for the salvation
> of his soul. Every particular act which furnishes even a pass-
> ing sense of gratification interferes with the certainty of
> eternal bliss and seems to lead to damnation.[15]

The second sonnet on fame is about the kind of fame achieved
in an afterlife by having lived on earth in a pure, Christian
manner. The idea is put forward that acceptance of the world
is a proper sort of wisdom. The poem warns against intemperate questioning of nature's processes and against questing
for worldly fame, which is called a "fierce miscreed." That the

---

[14] Wilhelm Stekel, *Auto-Erotism: A Psychiatric Study of Onanism and
Neurosis,* trans. by James S. Van Teslaar (New York, 1961), p. 239.
[15] *Ibid.,* p. 230.

sonnet propounds these ideas in figurative relationships having many sexual significations is important for an understanding of the emotional pressure of the poem. The intensity of the octave echoes what Keats calls in the letter preceding the poem the violence of his temperament, and the intensity is conveyed by the strong feelings shared by western man about masturbation.

Relief from the pressure of strong guilt feelings may have been provided by Keats's ideas about

> that which becks
> Our ready minds to fellowship divine.
>   ("Endymion," I, 777–78)

The first gradation on the pleasure thermometer (which may tell us how fevered the man is) includes roses, winds, impregnation, and a state of spiritual freedom. A tame and proper creed is stated in this passage:

> Behold
> The clear religion of heaven! Fold
> A rose leaf round thy finger's taperness,
> And soothe thy lips: hist, when the airy stress
> Of music's kiss impregnates the free winds,
> And with a sympathetic touch unbinds
> Eolian magic from their lucid wombs:
> Then old songs waken from enclouded tombs;
> Old ditties sigh above their father's grave;
> Ghosts of melodious prophecyings rave
> Round every spot where trod Apollo's foot;
> Bronze clarions awake, and faintly bruit,
> Where long ago a Giant Battle was;
> And, from the turf, a lullaby doth pass
> In every place where infant Orpheus slept.
> Feel we these things?—that moment have we stept
> Into a sort of oneness, and our state
> Is like a floating spirit's.
>   ("Endymion," I, 780–95)

Because nature is creative and has the power to reincarnate, sexuality is employed figuratively to describe man's quest for happiness and "fellowship divine" much as the rose and the wind function in the sonnet.

The sexual significations of the sonnet are thus seen to be a crucial part of Keats's religious philosophizing, a part expressed by submerged relationships that long remained in Keats's mind and poetry.

[7]

The Love of Death

What, not yet
Escap'd from dull mortality's harsh net?
("Endymion," III, 906–7.)

"Why did I laugh to-night?" also bears upon our interpretation of another of Keats's fundamental attitudes. Together with the very early lyric "On Death" it exposes a complex of relationships and emotions Keats never forsook, although his intellectual comprehension of death matured considerably.

In his discussion of the "Ode to a Nightingale" Bate cogently presents Keats's divided attitude toward death as it is available from the biography and the poetry.

> . . . Keats's constant exposure to death since the age of eight; the accumulated fatigue of the effort of the past four years; his uneasy feeling about his own future since he returned from Scotland with the 'haunting sore-throat.' Add to all this his attempts to manage this inevitable preoccupation with death. If a part of him tried to keep it out of his mind, another part instinctively tried to muffle the sense of cruelty and injustice, tending to reduce thoughts and symbols of death to the two attractions that so often alternate in his emotional life—'intensity' and 'easefulness'.[1]

---

[1] Bate, p. 507.

We can examine these two attractions in the letters as a prelude to considering their expression in the two poems. The aspect of intensity is glossed by Keats in his letter to his brothers of 21–27 December 1817 :

> I spent Friday evening with Wells & went the next morning to see *Death on The Pale Horse*. It is a wonderful picture, when West's age is considered ; But there is nothing to be intense upon ; no women one feels mad to kiss ; no face swelling into reality. the excellence of every Art is its intensity, capable of making all disagreeables evaporate, from their being in close relationship with Beauty & Truth.[2]

In the great journal letter in which he worked out his philosophy of disinterestedness and the vale of Soul-making, Keats considers the other attraction death offers.

> The whole appears to resolve into this—that Man is originally a 'poor forked creature' subject to the same mischances as the beasts of the forest, destined to hardships and disquietude of some kind or other. If he improves by degrees his bodily accomodations and comforts—at each stage, at each accent [sic] there are waiting for him a fresh set of annoyances— he is mortal and there is still a heaven with its Stars abov[e] his head. The most interesting question that can come before us is, How far by the persevering endeavours of a seldom appearing Socrates Mankind may be made happy—I can imagine such happiness carried to an extreme—but what must it end in ?—Death—and who could in such a case bear with death—the whole troubles of a life which are now frittered away in a series of years would the[n] be accumulated for the last days of a being who instead of hailing its approach, would leave this world as Eve left Paradise.[3]

It is Keats's contention that man must be as subservient to the world as a rose, which cannot escape or destroy the world's

---

[2] *Letters,* I, 192.

[3] *Ibid.,* II, 101.

annoyances because "they are as native to the world as itself: no more can man be happy in spite, the world[l]y elements will prey upon his nature."[4] Man must not, as Keats was shortly to write in the second sonnet on fame, torment or vex "all the leaves of his life's book" (line 3), and "Spoil his salvation for a fierce miscreed" (line 14). The point is that even though the example of the natural world shows the way to our salvation by objectifying the doctrine of the world as a vale of Soul-making, and leads to a rejection of egoism and an acceptance of disinterestedness, *nevertheless* death is easeful because it provides a respite from a "World of Pains and Troubles," "A Place where the heart must feel and suffer in a thousand diverse ways!"[5]

A similar attitude can be detected as early as "Endymion," where in book II, after following the naiad turned butterfly and learning that he

> must wander far
> In other regions, past the scanty bar
> To mortal steps, before thou cans't be ta'en
> From every wasting sigh, from every pain
> Into the gentle bosom of thy love,
>   ("Endymion," II, 124–27)

Endymion thinks:

> 'Whoso encamps
> To take a fancied city of delight
> O what a wretch is he! and when 'tis his,
> After long toil and travelling, to miss
> The kernel of his hopes, how more than vile:
> Yet for him there's refreshment even in toil;
> Another city doth he set about,
> Free from the smallest pebble-bead of doubt
> That he will seize on trickling honey-combs:

---

[4] *Ibid.*
[5] *Ibid.*, 102.

> Alas, he finds them dry; and then he foams,
> And onward to another city speeds.
> But this is human life: the war, the deeds,
> The disappointment, the anxiety,
> Imagination's struggles, far and nigh,
> All human, bearing in themselves this good,
> That they are still the air, the subtle food,
> To make us feel existence, and to show
> How quiet death is. Where soil is men grow,
> Whether to weeds or flowers.'
>
> ("Endymion," II, 142–59)

The germ of the vale of Soul-making idea is contained in the above passage, but the idea of easefulness is full-blown. Now we can begin to examine the complementary idea of intensity.

As we have seen, the sonnet "Why did I laugh to-night?" argues for death as a solution for the agony of ignorance despite Keats's knowledge of fancy's blisses and "this Being's lease"; death is a higher goal than the three great objects of Keats's quest:

> Verse, Fame, and Beauty are intense indeed,
> But Death intenser—Death is Life's high meed.
>
> (lines 13–14)

Ward also comments on Keats's preoccupation with death.

From the beginning his poetry had been shaped by his attempt somehow to escape from the realization of death; now he was finally relinquishing the attempt as meaningless. If the prospect of death was faced squarely, he saw, it could not be the negation of all the struggles of life but the supreme experience, 'intenser' than all the others in calling out all man's heroism to meet it. More than this, it might become 'life's high meed,' the resolution of all those doubts which can never be settled in life itself.[6]

---

[6] Ward, pp. 259–60.

What the critics overlook is that the attitude and language of the sonnet are practically identical to one of Keats's earliest poems, "On Death," where once again the notions of intensity and ease are coupled.

> Can death be sleep, when life is but a dream,
>   And scenes of bliss pass as a phantom by?
> The transient pleasures as a vision seem,
>   And yet we think the greatest pain's to die.
>
> How strange it is that man on earth should roam,
>   And lead a life of woe, but not forsake
> His rugged path; nor dare he view alone
>   His future doom, which is but to awake.

We can see at once that the pleasures of life, its *blisses,* are projected as being more intense after death (that is, when we are awake), more corporeal than in a dream. Death is "intenser." Death is more pleasurable than life for it will evaporate annoyances which, however educative, are annoyances. Our path here is rugged and strewn with woes, but the whole suggestion of the lyric is that in death things will be otherwise. Further, death will not call out heroism in the man who properly understands its non-dream kingdom, even though it exists only for those who do not need the strength of others to support them. I think we can see clearly that one of Keats's attitudes toward death, his longing for it, which opposes his ultimate rejection of it in the nightingale ode, persisted throughout his life while the reasons for the longing took on the tinge of his current philosophizing. This appears at last in the letter to Brown of 30 September 1820: "Is there another Life? Shall I awake and find all this a dream? There must be we cannot be created for this sort of suffering."[7]

As Walter Evert remarks, "It is unlikely that the 'Ode on

[7] *Letters,* II, 346.

Indolence' has ever been anyone's favorite poem,"[8] but this, of course, cannot diminish its importance. Robert Gittings has, rather obliquely, aligned the mood in which the ode was composed with the mood surrounding the composition of "Why did I laugh to-night?"[9], but far more than a mood is shared by the two poems. Claude Finney helps us to examine their relationship more closely:

> The *Ode on Indolence* does not present a new phase of Keats's criticism of life. It is little more than a metrical paraphrase of that fit of apathy which he described in the journal letter to his brother on March 19, 1819. He considered the three chief problems of his experience—poetry, ambition, and love—in the sonnet *Why did I laugh tonight?* which he composed on March 19 or a day or two thereafter. He considered the problem of ambition in the two sonnets *On Fame,* which he composed on April 30; and he considered the problem of love in a series of poems which he composed in the latter half of April—the sonnets *As Hermes Once,* and *Bright Star!,* the second ode *To [Fanny],* and the ballad *La Belle dame.* And he considered the problem of poetry both philosophically and technically in his letters and in his poems. Although he mastered the painful truths of life and accepted them with stoical fortitude, he welcomed sleep and mental apathy; which gave him a momentary relief from pain, and death, which would give him complete and final relief.[10]

Careful examination will show that Finney is wrong in suggesting that the ode does not represent an advance in Keats's thought, for the sonnet and the ode provide alternative solutions.

The problem presented in the sonnet and the ode is the choosing of that mode of existence—or nonexistence—which will provide the greatest intensity. In each poem there are three candidates for the position of quest-figure: the sonnet names

---

[8] Evert, p. 305.

[9] *Living Year,* pp. 101–2.

[10] Finney, II, 647—48.

them Verse, Fame, and Beauty; the ode calls them Poesy, Ambition, and Love. The sonnet dismisses the abstractions—phantoms?—because they do not possess sufficient intensity when compared to death.

> Verse, Fame, and Beauty are intense indeed,
> But Death intenser—Death is Life's high meed.
> (lines 13–14)

We have already noticed that Keats often considered death as "easeful" and "intense."[11] That indolence is roughly the same as the state of easeful death is also discoverable in the letters. The description of the symptoms of his indolence in the journal letter is saturated with easefulness and near unconsciousness. Further, the state is linked with death because the reverie was interrupted by news of impending death, and the thought of death immediately precedes it:

> Yesterday I got a black eye . . . This is the second black eye I have had since leaving school—during all my [scho]ol days I never had one at all—we must e[a]t a peck before we die—This morning I am in a sort of temper indolent and supremely careless: I long after a stanza or two of Thompson's Castle of Indolence—My passions are all asleep from my having slumbered till nearly eleven and weakened the animal fibre all over me to a delightful sensation about three degrees on this side of faintness—if I had teeth of pearl and the breath of lillies I should call it languor—but as I am I must call it Laziness—In this state of effeminacy the fibres of the brain are relaxed in common with the rest of the body, and to such a happy degree that pleasure has no show of enticement and pain no unbearable frown. Neither Poetry, nor Ambition, nor Love have any alertness of countenance as they pass by me: they seem rather like three figures on a greek vase—a Man and two women—whom no one but myself could distinguish in their disguisement. This is the

---

11 For a collection of references to death as an affective state and the development of the idea in the odes, see Van Ghent, pp. 26–32.

only happiness; and is a rare instance of advantage in the body overpowering the Mind. I have this moment received a note from Haslam in which he expects the death of his Father—who has been for sometime in a state of insensibility.[12]

Furthermore, in the sonnet to Reynolds, "What the Thrush Said," which praises indolence as productive of knowledge, we notice the appearance of a familiar relationship, the one we have traced back as far as the very early lyric "On Death." The thrush concludes: "And he's awake who thinks himself asleep" (line 14), which is one way of saying that sensations will be more intense after death. The letter to Bailey of 22 November 1817 glosses this idea: Life, Keats writes,

is 'a Vision in the form of Youth' a Shadow of reality to come—and this consideration has further conv[i]nced me for it has come as auxiliary to another favorite Speculation of mine, that we shall enjoy ourselves hereafter by having what we call happiness on Earth repeated in a finer tone[13] and so repeated—And yet such a fate can only befall those who delight in sensation rather than hunger as you do after Truth.[14]

This rich death, which, in the sonnet, is thought to be "Life's highest meed," is first accepted, then rejected in the "Ode on Indolence." The first turning point occurs in the fifth stanza:

> They faded, and, forsooth! I wanted wings:
>   O folly! What is Love! And where is it?

---

[12] *Letters,* II, 78–9.
[13] This is versified in "Endymion", IV, 849–54.

> I would have thee my only friend, sweet maid!
> My only visitor! not ignorant though,
> That those deceptions which for pleasures go
> Mong men, are pleasures real as real may be:
> But there are higher ones I may not see,
> If impiously an earthly realm I take.

[14] *Letters,* I, 185.

> And for that poor Ambition! it springs
>   From a man's little heart's short fever-fit;
> For Poesy!—no,—she has not a joy,—
>   At least for me,—so sweet as drowsy noons,
>   And evenings steep'd in honied indolence;
>   O for an age so shelter'd from annoy,
>   That I may never know how change the moons,
>   Or hear the voice of busy common-sense![15]

The goals symbolized by the three figures are rejected in
stanza five in favor of death, which, together with the other
three, is in turn rejected for reality in stanza six.

> So, ye three ghosts, adieu! Ye cannot raise
>   My head cool-bedded in the flowery grass;
> For I would not be dieted with praise,
>   A pet-lamb in a sentimental farce!
> Fade softly from my eyes, and be once more
>   In masque-like figures on the dreamy urn;
>   Farewell! I yet have visions for the night,
>   And for the day faint visions there is store;
>   Vanish, ye Phantoms! from my idle spright,
>   Into the clouds, and never more return!

Bate recalls the biographical circumstances at the time of
composition in order to account for the ending of the ode.

> Was he really surrendering very much, therefore, if he
> signed up as a ship's surgeon for a year or two? True, he
> had received praise and expectation aplenty from a small
> circle of kindly friends. But this was no assurance that he
> was not simply another poetaster who, like Hunt, was 'de-
> luding' himself. ('There is no greater Sin after the 7 deadly

---

[15] This is roughly equivalent to the state into which Venus has placed
Adonis in "Endymion," II, 484–86. Venus medicined death to a
lengthened drowsiness

> The which she fills with visions, and doth dress
> In all this quiet luxury.

than to flatter oneself into an idea of being a great Poet.')
No, these three figures in the ode whom he was preparing to
dismiss were as unattainable, as fundamentally unreal, as
those figures on that other Grecian Urn that he had been unable to join. Let them be regarded as what they were—mere
figures.[16]

So the "Ode on Indolence" does propose a fundamentally
different solution to one of Keats's familiar problems. The
speaker posits the problem, rejects a solution we found pro-
pounded in another poem, and announces his acceptance of a
new alternative.

---

[16] Bate, p. 530.

[8]

The Death of Love

The reality Keats intended to accept as his new alternative had
already been projected, though in a poem recording a dream.
This method of retaining the best of both possible worlds is
not unusual in Keats's poetry; as Professor Perkins reminds
us, "Even in *The Fall of Hyperion,* where the escapist dreamer
is reproached, the form of the poem is still a dream vision."[1]
As is so often the case, the letter in which the poem is contained
glosses the poem. By explicitly presenting contrasts whose details are submerged in the sonnet "On a Dream," the following
extract from the journal letter to the George Keatses provides
another example of the poet's philosophical development and
sophistication.

> The fifth canto of Dante pleases me more and more—it is
> that one in which he meets with Paulo and Franc[h]esca—I
> had passed many days in rather a low state of mind and in the
> midst of them I dreamt of being in that region of Hell. The
> dream was one of the most delightful enjoyments I ever had
> in my life—I floated about the whirling atmosphere as it is
> described with a beautiful figure to whose lips mine were
> joined at it seem'd for an age—and in the midst of all this
> cold and darkness I was warm—even flowery tree tops
> sprung up and we rested on them sometimes with the light-
> ness of a cloud till the wind blew us away again—I tried

[1] p. 192. This was also noted by Thorpe and Ford, both on p. 145.

a Sonnet upon it—there are fourteen lines but nothing of
what I felt in it—o that I could dream it every night—

> As Hermes once took to his feathers light
> When lulled Argus, baffled, swoon'd and slept
> So on a delphic reed by idle spright
> So play'd, so charm'd, so conquer'd, so bereft
> The dragon world of all its hundred eyes
> And seeing it asleep so fled away :—
> Not to pure Ida with its snow [clad] cold skies,
> Nor unto Tempe where Jove grieved that day,
> But to that second circle of sad hell,
> Where in the gust, the whirlwind and the flaw
> Of Rain and hailstones lovers need not tell
> Their sorrows—Pale were the sweet lips I saw
> Pale were the lips I kiss'd and fair the fo[r]m
> I floated with about that melancholy storm—[2]

Keats's "idle spright" fled to a realm where pain and joy
coalesce into a single experience and where the "annoys" of the
world are maturely accepted as a part of the process of Soul-
making. We ought to recall now that it is Keats's "idle spright"
from whom the ghosts or phantoms were dismissed in the "Ode
on Indolence."

> Vanish, ye Phantoms! from my idle spright
> Into the clouds, and never more return.
> (lines 59–60)

Through the device of lulling the hundred-eyed dragon world,
what was called in the ode "the voice of busy common sense"
(line 50) is banished. We can see an attempt here to make the
dream world more real by saying that the world was asleep,
yet we are aware that the poem is about a dream. This motif
of sleep's (or death's) providing greater sensuous awareness is
one we have already examined. Regardless, we can see that the

---

[2] *Letters,* II, 91.

poem equates a dream state with the realm of the imagination, and it shows that there can exist dreams that picture an attainable brave new world as well as those that proffer vain, deluding joys.

The speaker in the ode experienced a sleep "embroider'd with dim dreams" (line 22) but, in dismissing the three ghosts, claims

> I yet have visions for the night,
> And for the day faint visions there is store.
>   (lines 57–58)

One of these is the dream vision of Paolo and Francesca who, like the poet, forever share their love in the midst of hell.

As I have reiterated, the sonnet "On a Dream" presents a vision of reality that offers some hope of attainment because in it joy coexists with disagreeables. But we have not yet traced to its end this brightening path, for another poem springing from the same source needs to be considered in conjunction with the sonnet, as Gittings has shown. Writing of the sonnet, he observes:

> Nor was this the only poem in manuscript to be influenced by these cantos and this translation of the *Inferno* at this time. About a week later, on April 21st, and in the same letter to George Keats, there appears the first draft of the famous *La Belle Dame Sans Merci*. Many threads have spun together in the making of this magical poem, and even if all were to be traced, the work would still remain a miracle. Yet there is clearly some connection between the sonnet's

> Pale were the sweet lips I saw
> Pale were the lips I kiss'd and the fair form

and the lyric's two most evocative stanzas, which in their first draft read:

> I saw pale Kings and Princes too
> Pale warriors death pale were they all

They cried La belle dame sans merci
Thee hath in thrall.

I saw their starv'd lips in the gloam
  All ~~tremble~~
                gaped
With horrid warning/wide ~~agape~~
And I awoke and found me here
  On the cold hill's side.

The connection is that both owe a great deal to Canto V
of the *Inferno,* and to Francesca's story beginning

> "Love, that in gentle heart is quickly learnt,
> Entangled him by that fair form,

It was the most famous lines of that story that so influenced
Keats, as they have done everyone who reads them:

One day

For our delight we read of Lancelot,
How him love thrall'd. Alone we were, and no
Suspicion near us. Ofttimes by that reading
Our eyes were drawn together, and the hue
Fled from our alter'd cheek. But at one point
Alone we fell. When of that smile we read,
The wished smile, so rapturously kiss'd
By one so deep in love, then he, who ne'er
From me shall separate, at once my lips
All trembling kiss'd.[3]

There is more to be said about the two poems, for we can
detect beneath the similarity of diction a functional relationship. If, for a moment, the speaker in "On a Dream" and the
knight in "La Belle Dame" can be considered as variations of a
man questing for love, we see that the dream vision of unalter-
ing love in the sonnet, which was an alternative to the re-

---

[3] *Mask of Keats,* pp. 30–31.

jected vision of love in the ode, turned out not to be viable despite the inclusion of disagreeables.[4] The reasons are complex, but not unfamiliar. Bate and Wasserman agree on the causes, and shed a great deal of light on Keats's most mature perception of the conflict between the ideal and the real. Bate writes on the end of the ballad,

> Finally, though the ultimate impossibility of contact between the human and this elusive, only half human figure is premised throughout, no suggestion that she is sinister is made except through the subjective response of the knight's own imagination. He himself does not actually witness the 'horrid warning' of starvation that this attempted union might bring. That anticipation, which may be genuine or primarily the expression of his own uneasiness, has come to him only in a dream— a dream that has also banished 'la belle dame.' And if the dream is now proving to be prophetic, it is again through his own divided nature, his own act. . . .[5]

It seems plain that the figures of the woman in the sonnet and the ballad are similarly vague and elusive, not fully human. This taint of immortality is crucial, as Wasserman suggests in his analysis of the end of the ballad.

> It is man's bond with mankind that prevents him from lingering beyond the bourne of care. There is nothing in Keats's ballad even suggesting the frequent interpretation that the fairy's child is responsible for the knight's expulsion from the elfin grot; only his own inherent attribute of being mortal causes his magic withdrawal. . . . The vision of the mortal-immortal can only entice man towards heaven's bourne; it cannot aid him in his aspirations or preserve his vision, which

---

[4] For a more biographically oriented interpretation, which silently owes much to Gittings, see Pettet, pp. 218–19. Douglas Bush's brief comment on "As Hermes once" is worth noting: "This sonnet had described a dream he wished he could have every night; its obverse side appears in *La Belle Dame*." (Bush, p. 124)

[5] Bate, pp. 480—81.

must inevitably be shattered. By this fair enchantment mortal man can only be 'tortured with renewed life.' ["Endymion," I, 919][6]

That is, when applied to the sonnet as well, not even the admission of "annoys," or disagreeables, into the ideal world can long save one from having to make the "journey homeward to habitual self." Perhaps the "Ode on Indolence" shows an attempt and a failure to re-establish faith in the ideal state like the one posited in the dream sonnet, but which Keats had already rejected as specious in "La Belle Dame."

As I state in the appendix to this study, I am in general agreement with Walter Evert's techniques and conclusions in his discussion of Endymion's defense of "the authenticity of love and imagination as modes of achieving a 'self-destroying' spiritual reality which beggars that inferior kind centered in a consciousness of selfhood in the substantive world."[7] Evert finds the "anti-theme" of the episode in "La Belle Dame" in "Endymion," and points out many of the important similarities in the situations and in the language Keats used to describe and discuss them. But one that he ignored is crucial in interpreting the significance of the "past victims" of the "evil enchantress," a subject on which he disagrees with Wasserman is a nearly unintelligible footnote.[8] Where Wasserman finds the kings, princes, and warriors to be negative and intrusive symbols of life, Evert argues that the figures "do not intrude on the rapturous interlude with the fairy's child but appear as warning figures in a sleeping dream."[9] The knight is beyond our moral judgment while asleep, Evert claims, and so we cannot say he is weak in failing to remain in his dream realm. Evert

---

[6] Wasserman, pp. 74–75.

[7] Evert, pp. 252–53.

[8] *Ibid.,* p. 254.

[9] *Ibid.*

further objects to Wasserman's identification of the warning figures "with worldly 'Men of Power,' an expression used by Keats a year-and-a-half earlier to designate 'Those who have a proper self' [*Letters*, I, 184]."[10]

Evert might have strengthened his argument had he elaborated on another part of the relationship between the poems. In arguing for the validity of fellowship with essence, or "the holiness of the heart's affections when they are made correlative with the truth of imagination,"[11] Endymion speaks of

> Men, who might have tower'd in the van
> Of all the congregated world, to fan
> And winnow from the coming step of time
> All chaff of custom, wipe away all slime
> Left by men-slugs and human serpentry,
> Have been content to let occasion die,
> Whilst they did sleep in love's elysium.
> And truly, I would rather be struck dumb,
> Than speak against this ardent listlessness.
> For I have ever thought that it might bless
> The world with benefits unknowingly;
> As does the nightingale, upperched high,
> And cloister'd among cool and bunched leaves—
> She sings but to her love, nor e'er conceives
> How tip-toe night holds back her dark-grey hood.
> Just so may love, although 'tis understood
> The mere commingling of passionate breath,
> Produce more than our searching witnesseth:

---

[10] *Ibid.* Stanley C. Russell has recently discovered another way in which love robs man of what might be considered a "proper self." He argues that in Keats's "intense desire . . . to maintain his identity . . . the clue to his conception of love as 'self-destroying' is to be found." Self-destruction ought not be thought of as akin to negative capability because "Negative capability was something desirable. It was the agent which he felt would free his artistic powers from their mortal bondage. But sexual love was a threat to his self-possession and his will to create." " 'Self-Destroying' Love in Keats," *K-SJ*, XVI (1967), 77–91. Both quotations appear on p. 83.

[11] *Ibid.*, p. 256.

What I know not: but who, of men, can tell
That flowers would bloom, or that green fruit would swell
To melting pulp, that fish would have bright mail,
The earth its dower of river, wood, and vale,
The meadows runnels, runnels pebble-stones,
The seed its harvest, or the lute its tones,
Tones ravishment, or ravishment its sweet,
If human souls did never kiss and greet?
("Endymion," I, 817–42)

Endymion argues that even those men who could have been of greater value to mankind than kings, princes, and warriors have quite properly accepted total identification with love and its realm; they have quite properly rejected worldly power, for in the end this identification is productive of even greater good to mankind. They are great spirits not on earth sojourning.

That such men appear in "Endymion" shows Keats's awareness of the pressure of the counter-theme of the real world at this early stage in his speculations. In "La Belle Dame" he answers the question posed in "Endymion": he tells which men will deny that acceptance of love in an ideal realm is a greater good. I suggest that the point is that even kings and princes and warriors realize the falsity of the ideal realm, but there is surely a plausible argument that only this sort of man is too weak to give the total commitment the realm requires.

The brief lyric, "Unfelt, unheard, unseen," was probably composed in November, 1817, about a year and a half before "La Belle Dame sans Merci." Despite the neglect accorded it, it is an important poem presenting an alternative ending to the familiar story of a debilitating love which, as many have pointed out, is so common in Keats's poetry.

Unfelt, unheard, unseen,
I've left my little queen,
Her languid arms in silver slumber lying:

Ah! through their nestling touch,
Who—who could tell how much
There is for madness—cruel, or complying?

Those faery lids how sleek!
Those lips how moist!—they speak,
In ripest quiet, shadows of sweet sounds:
Into my fancy's ear
Melting a burden dear,
How 'Love doth know no fullness nor no bounds.'

True! tender monitors!
I bend unto your laws:
This sweetest day for dalliance was born!
So, without more ado,
I'll feel my heaven anew,
For all the blushing of the hasty morn.

Sidney Colvin finds the stanzas to be "very daintily finished," though he cannot agree with Mary Suddard that the poem is the first of Keats's "technically faultless achievements."[12] Aileen Ward thinks the poem is part of a "little group of love lyrics which express all the moods of a summer romance," "Unfelt, unheard, unseen" expressing "tender farewell."[13] Walter Jackson Bate thinks the poem and its companion, "Think not of it sweet one," were written to provide relief from the tedious form of "Endymion," but concludes that "they provided no relief; their very triviality shows how preoccupied he was if not with *Endymion* itself, at least with the need to get it done."[14]

Amy Lowell provides the only comments of any length on the two poems, and her comments in part anticipate Bate's.

There is no merit in either of these poems. They read like

---

[12] Colvin, p. 157.
[13] Ward, p. 124.
[14] Bate, p. 228.

exercises of lyric form rather than anything else. But, also, they seem an attempt to catch a gossamer beauty, a sort of beauty quite foreign to the type with which Keats had been busy for months. Needless to say, they fail, drooping weakly to the ground not undraggled by the sticky sweetness of Keats's early work. The last things they seem are records of any real occurrence. I am forced to the conclusion that they are simply and solely experiments on Keats's part to see if he had lost his versatility, and a sort of mental outlet to his brain, overworked with one point of view and, with the exception of the *Indian Maiden's Song*, one metre.[15]

The hypothesis that it was the form rather than the subject of the poem which Keats was most conscious of at the time of composition does not preclude the subject's importance. It makes it all the more likely that the subject would be a familiar one, or one aspect of or one approach to a subject that was continually present in the poet's unconscious. That this is probable may be seen by a comparison of "Unfelt, unheard, unseen" and "La Belle Dame sans Merci." I should like to begin by quoting Earl Wasserman's analysis of the theme of "La Belle Dame" because part of his conclusion leaves room for analysis of the relationships I wish to explore.

Professor Wasserman finds that the lady is without tenderness not because she is cruel, but because it is her nature to provoke man's aspiration toward heaven's bourne:

> Like the lady of the tradition of courtly love, she is the ideal whom the lover must pursue but whom he can never possess; and hence he is doomed to suffer her 'unkindness,' which is her nature although not her fault. Only the inherent meanness of man's dreams, then, draws him back from heaven's bourne, for, instead of being visionary penetrations into that final essence which is beauty-truth, they are only of mutable things. Aspire though he will, the stings of human neighborhood envenom all.[16]

15 Lowell, I, 520.
16 Wasserman, p. 75.

Further, Wasserman finds that "La Belle Dame" and the "Ode on a Grecian Urn"

> are variant artistic intertextures of the three coexistent themes that dominate Keats's deepest meditations and profoundest system of values: the oxymoronic heaven's bourne toward which his spirit yearned; the pleasure thermometer which he conceived of as the spiritual path to that goal; and the self-annihilation he understood to be the condition necessary for the journey.[17]

Wasserman finds too that "In his discovery that art prefigures an attainable heaven where beauty will be truth, Keats spoke to man an Everlasting Yea; 'La Belle Dame Sans Merci' in his center of Indifference."[18] I find that "Unfelt, unheard, unseen" is "La Belle Dame" as Everlasting Yea.

In the first three lines of the lyric we are told that the speaker almost incorporeally has left his "little queen" slumbering. At least two elements of "La Belle Dame" are present: the heightening of significance gained by choosing royalty as *dramatis personae*,[19] and the fact that one of the partners is asleep. The lack of sensation provides an aura of enchantment. The next three lines are an exclamation and a question: the touch of the woman's arms, which is to say, love, deprives the speaker—and by extension all of us—of rational judgment, but we learn too that the judgment is of things irrational:

> Who—who could tell how much
> There is for madness—cruel or complying?

The loss of the power to reason as a consequence of love can bode good or ill, but it will surely occur and the speaker is aware of the risk he is taking.

---

[17] *Ibid.*, p. 83.

[18] *Ibid.*

[19] These similarities, though minor, are not trivial. Like the triad of images appearing in "Sleep and Poetry" and "Ode to a Nightingale," the recurrences themselves demonstrate nothing. However, their presence signals us that more important relationships are shared by the poems. Compare the comments on pages 69 and 70.

The second stanza also shares a number of relationships with "La Belle Dame." The eyes of the "little queen" have sleek "faery lids." Although her eyes are not described as wild, the possibility exists that she too is "Full beautiful, a faery's child" (line 14). Her moist lips are the next anatomical part mentioned. These are, let us recall, a queen's lips, and momentarily they will speak delicately; so they are, like the lips in "La Belle Dame," royal lips capable of speech, and the sound they emit is no less true. The queen's lips form "In ripest quiet, shadows of sweet sounds." Imagery of ripeness is present at the beginning of "La Belle Dame" where we learn that

> The squirrel's granary is full
> And the harvest's done.
> (lines 7–8)

Furthermore, this stanza suggests that these "shadows of sweet sounds" *melt* a "burden" into the ear of the speaker's fancy. The burden is no less important as a stylistic device than for what it says, for a burden is a repeated line or group of lines, and as such it is not only characteristic of the ballad form but also an integral component of the structure of the ballad we are considering. The actual statement, "Love doth know no fullness nor no bounds" quite possibly describes the sort of thralldom or total commitment that love for la belle dame requires: recall that in "When I have fears" the speaker regrets that he may never have relish in "the faery power of unreflecting love" (lines 11–12). This sort of totality of commitment ignores the tension of opposites that is a sign of maturity in Keats's later poems, but which is, as we have so frequently seen, uncharacteristic of his early poetry which largely ignores the stings of human neighborhood, or, as David Perkins has put it, which makes "no attempt to reconcile . . . desires with the world of limited possibilities in which we live."[20] Nevertheless, "Unfelt, unheard, unseen," at least considers the claims of the real world where such commitment to love or the realm

[20] Perkins, p. 191.

of the imagination may be seen to be harmful, even though these claims are finally rejected.

It is important to notice the relationships the second stanza shares with another of Keats's major poems on the theme of love, "The Eve of St. Agnes," especially stanzas thirty-one to thirty-three. There the banquet scene presents us another picture of ripest quiet and shadows of sweet sounds. The luxurious foods are heaped in their rich baskets where

> sumptuous they stand
> In the retired quiet of the night,
> Filling the chilly room with perfume light.
> > (lines 273–75)

Madeline's dream is "impossible to *melt*" (line 283, emphasis supplied), but Porphyro takes up her hollow lute

> and, in chords that tenderest be,
> He play'd an ancient ditty, long since mute,
> In Provence call'd, "La belle dame sans mercy."
> > (lines 290–92)

The third stanza of "Unfelt, unheard, unseen," states emphatically that the burden of the lips is "True!" Apparently this suggests that if this love contains elements of madness, they are not cruel, but complying; not evil but good. In fact, the coming of the "hasty morn," which might easily have served to trigger an awakening into the world of reality, is deliberately ignored as a warning, the speaker choosing to "feel my heaven anew" in a day born for "dalliance." The courtly significations of "dalliance" place us once again in the world of "La Belle Dame," and the ominous threat of a cruel madness makes its final appearance. Nevertheless, the real world will not impinge; heaven—symbolically heaven's bourne—having been attained can and will be retained.

Thus once again we find an early poem specifically presenting total penetration into the realm of the visionary imagination, a condition which later poems postulate but argue cannot be maintained. Again I suggest that the constancy of the symbolic counters, the imagery of harvests, faeries, delicate sounds, eyes and lips, the themes of enchantment, cruelty, and a total commitment to love, that to find all of these expressed in similar relationships is not surprising or unusual in the works of a poet who continually worked out in poetry alternative solutions to his central dilemmas. Once again the tenacity of certain relationships is established, as is the tendency to let part of a habitual relationship function for the whole. Just as surely as this poem is not one of tender farewell, it is not trivial.

The first "Ode to Fanny" ("Physician Nature! let my spirit blood!") was composed at least two, possibly three years after the lyric "You say you love," which may have been written to Isabella Jones. Regardless of the dates or addressees,[21] the poems exhibit relationships linking them more clearly than anyone has yet pointed out. Both poems suggest how a lover ought to be treated by his mistress, and both are concerned with how a mistress ought not treat her lover, or how she ought to respond to the attentions of other suitors. The two poems use similar relationships to present the attitudes, and once again the constancy and tenacity of the relationships and significations that cluster around a dynamic situation demonstrate its profound importance to Keats.

The lyric consists of five stanzas each of which is concerned primarily with suggesting an attitude by means of a single relationship. The first four stanzas suggest new attitudes by deprecating the one presented by the relationship. The final stanza suggests what a proper attitude would be.

I

You say you love; but with a voice
Chaster than a nun's, who singeth

---

[21] For information on these topics consult Colvin, p. 157; Finney, I, 191, II, 544–45; Lowell, I, 112; and Gittings, *Mask of Keats,* p. 50.

The soft vespers to herself
  While the chime-bell ringeth—
    O love me truly!

II

You say you love; but with a smile
  Cold as sunrise in September,
As you were Saint Cupid's nun,
  And kept his weeks of Ember.
    O love me truly!

III

You say you love—but then your lips
  Coral tinted teach no blisses,
More than coral in the sea—
  They never pout for kisses—
    O love me truly!

IV

You say you love; but then your hand
  No soft squeeze for squeeze returneth,
It is like a Statue's, dead,—
  While mine to passion burneth—
    O love me truly!

V

O breathe a word or two of fire!
  Smile, as if those words should burn me,
Squeeze as lovers should—O kiss
  And in thy heart inurn me!
    O love me truly!

The "Ode to Fanny" consist of seven stanzas. The first is an
invocation and is not germane to this study. The remaining six
stanzas are Keats's imaginings of how Fanny might be acting
and responding at the dance she is attending, and they contain
injunctions to her to respond in certain ways to the attentions
of others if she truly loves Keats.

Although they do not occur in the same order in the two
poems, similar relationships are used to suggest or express
proper attitudes. For example, in the lyric the woman's voice is
"chaster than a nun's," and this is not at all suggestive of the
kind of warmth and devotion that the speaker thinks love re-

quires. But Fanny is urged to act as decorously as a nun, for she is, to her lover, not only nun-like but "My Holy See of love" (line 51), a "sacramental cake" (line 53). It would seem that in trying to suggest how dispassionately he thought Fanny should act, Keats leaned over too far backward, as it were, for Fanny in these lines does not seem to be animate; she is a shrine, not a worshiper.

In the second stanza of the lyric we learn that the woman's smile belies her declaration of love. It is

> Cold as a sunrise in September
> As you were Saint Cupid's nun,
> And kept his weeks of Ember.

Fanny is urged, in stanza IV of the ode, to

> Be like an April day,
> Smiling and cold and gay,

in order that Keats may have a "warmer June" (lines 28–29, 32). It is worth noticing that Ember days occur four times during the year, corresponding roughly to the seasonal changes. They need not occur in April, for they are celebrated on the first Sunday after Easter, or May 15 or 26. Nevertheless, the suggestion of seasonal change is implicit in the significations of April as they are used in the ode. Further, in the stanza there is another religious signification appearing in the wish that Fanny would act like "a temperate lily, temperate as fair" (line 30).

The sea is the basis of relationships in both poems. Though the precise significations alter the relationships, they are both oriented negatively; they represent a rejection of extremes: the woman ought not behave like coral or like a feather.

> You say you love; but then your lips
> Coral-tinted teach no blisses,
> More than coral in the sea—
> They never pout for kisses.

Fanny is told to confess that she possesses a woman's nature, one changeable and unstable. The speaker asks (hoping the answer will be "no")

> Must not a woman be
> A feather on the sea,
> Sway'd to and fro by every wind and tide?
> (lines 32–34)

The woman-sea relationship is continued from stanza III where Keats asks that the "current of her [Fanny's] heart" (line 22) not be diverted from him to others. This water imagery may have been introduced into the poem because of an association with fire, or warmth. Keats has mentioned suitors who "amorous burn" (line 20), who are, we might suppose, like Hermes "bent warm on amorous theft" ("Lamia," line 8). Further, the idea of warmth is present in the ode and the end of the following stanza where, as we have already noted, Keats asks for a "Warmer June." Additionally, in the autograph manuscript there is a canceled line at the beginning of stanza II that reads, "My temples with hot jealous pulses beat." But if this is a destructive fire, there is, if not a constructive one, at least one less painful. The relationship of warmth, burning, and heart occurs again in the final stanza of the lyric.

Thus we see that Keats's projections of the proper attitudes for a lover to take did not vary from time to time, and the relationships in which they achieved their expression did not change either. It is interesting too that the relationships were used negatively, in the sense that they indicate undesirable attitudes for a mistress to take toward her lover, although they would be correct if adopted toward other suitors. It does not seem unfair to conjecture that attitudes some early wished-for mistress held toward Keats made a lasting impression, and did not cease to give pain when they were directed—perhaps not maliciously but flirtatiously—by Fanny Brawne.

[9]

The Wideness of the Sea

The sea meant much to Keats as a symbol containing and expressing the limitless possibilities held by the future. Many of the possibilities were bright: a career as a poet, a glorious afterfame, a promise of insight into the immutable laws of nature; but others were dark; he had thoughts of an "eternal fierce destruction," of his inability fully to explore the sea's mysterious isles, and of being speechless—unknown—throughout eternity. Not all of Keats's poems or parts of poems dealing with the sea[1] provide more than precise descriptions or settings of heightened significance, but many exhibit his ability to choose significations that precisely convey a particular feeling. Usually this feeling is a compound of emotions stimulated by uncertainty as to which possibilities would be realized. This can be seen in the first of the poems I shall discuss, the sonnet "To My Brother George," where one of the day's wonders Keats writes of is

> The ocean, with its vastness, its blue green,
> Its ships, its rocks, its caves, its hopes, its fears—
> Its voice mysterious which whoso hears
> Must think on what will be, and what has been.
>
> (lines 5–8)

Anxiety about the future is no small part of the feeling of these

---
1 For a convenient list, consult DeSelincourt, p. 541.

lines. Finney perceptively contrasts this description of the sea
with the one in the epistle "To my Brother George."

> And on the other side, outspread, is seen
> Ocean's blue mantle streak'd with purple, and green.
> Now 'tis I see a canvass'd ship, and now
> Mark the bright silver curling round her prow.
> I see the lark down-dropping to his nest,
> And the broad winged sea-gull never at rest;
> For when no more he spreads his feathers free,
> His breast is dancing on the restless sea.
>
> (lines 131–38)

Finney comments:

> The sonnet glows with the wonder of natural beauty which
> was perceived directly and felt vividly; but, unlike the de-
> scription in the epistle, which was composed from direct ob-
> servation in the afternoon, it was composed in recollection
> in the evening; and his mind, which was pregnant with poetic
> lore, enriched his experience of natural beauty with fancies,
> feelings, reflections, and reminiscences. The style of descrip-
> tion in the sonnet, therefore, is quite different from that in
> the epistle. To use Hazlitt's distinction, the scene in the
> sonnet was described less from the eye and more from the
> mind than the scene in the epistle.[2]

Amy Lowell also comments on the emotional power of the
sonnet, saying, "The remarkable thing about this passage is
that it not only paints the actual sea, but suggests all that the
sea stands for to humanity, and this with no effect of over-
loading and spoiling the picture."[3]

The next poem (the order in this section is chronological)
in which Keats uses the sea as the sort of symbol I am tracing
is the Chapman's *Homer* sonnet. The feeling Keats had upon

---

[2] Finney, I, 119.
[3] Lowell, I, 159.

breathing the "pure serene" of Chapman's translation he compares to that of

> Stout Cortez when with eagle eyes
> He star'd at the Pacific—and all his men
> Look'd at each other with a wild surmise—
> Silent, upon a peak in Darien.
>
> (lines 11–14)

A discovery has been made, both by Cortez and by his men, but there must still be "wild surmise," for the Pacific, or the "wide expanse," is so vast that nothing definite or concrete can be ascertained or felt, but only surmises, conjectures based on scanty evidence. The enormity, the vastness of the discovery permits no single, uncontaminated emotion to be felt, but rather it provokes ambivalent feelings, hopes and fears, and this amalgam of feeling is so powerfully suggested by Keats that the sonnet stands among the greatest attempts to express the feeling of the human condition.

"Sleep and Poetry" presents the attractiveness and the fearsomeness of the sea in even more fragmented form, and the speaker there, debating a career in poetry, feels alternately the two poles of the magnet, finally refusing to unsay his wish for

> ten years that I may overwhelm
> Myself in poesy.
>
> (lines 96–97)

He argues that his clear vision of "The end and aim of Poesy" (line 293) compels him to speak out what he has dared to think. At first he would plunge into poetry rather than, like a coward, shrink from what he conceives to be his destiny.

> Ah! rather let me like a madman run
> Over some precipice; let the hot sun
> Melt my Dedalian wings, and drive me down
> Convuls'd and headlong!
>
> (lines 301–4)

This uncontrolled descent is apparently what some critics think happened to Keats in "Endymion," where, as Keats wrote to Hessey,

> I leaped headlong into the Sea,[4] and thereby have become better acquainted with the Soundings, the quicksands, & the rocks, than if I had stayed upon the green shore, and piped a silly pipe, and took tea & comfortable advice.—I was never afraid of failure; for I would sooner fail than not be among the greatest—But I am nigh getting into a rant.[5]

The lines that follow in "Sleep and Poetry" contain more of the familiar amalgam of attraction and repulsion, and the abruptness of the speaker's decision indicates the wildness of his surmises as well as his estimate of their prospects of becoming real.

> Stay! an inward frown
> Of conscience bids me be more calm awhile.
> An ocean dim, sprinkled with many an isle,
> Spreads awfully before me. How much toil!
> How many days! what desperate turmoil!
> Ere I can have explored its widenesses.
> Ah, what a task! upon my bended knees,
> I could unsay those—no, impossible!
> Impossible!
>
> (lines 304–12)

The sonnet "On the Sea" was written during a time of doubt and uncertainty prior to the beginning of work on "Endymion."

> It keeps eternal whisperings around
>   Desolate shores, and with its mighty swell
>   Gluts twice ten thousand caverns, till the spell
> Of Hecate leaves them their old shadowy sound.

---

[4] Endymion himself stood "upon a misty, jutting head of land" (II, 163).
[5] *Letters*, I, 374.

Often 'tis in such gentle temper found
  That scarcely will the very smallest shell
  Be moved for days from where it sometime fell,
When last the winds of heaven were unbound.
Oh ye! who have your eye-balls vexed and tired,
  Feast them upon the wideness of the Sea;
Oh ye! whose ears are dinn'd with uproar rude,
  Or fed too much with cloying melody—
Sit ye near some old cavern's mouth, and brood
Until ye start, as if the sea nymphs quired!

Keats included the sonnet in a letter written in the Isle of Wight and addressed to Reynolds.

Shanklin is a most beautiful place—sloping wood and meadow ground reaches round the Chine, which is a cleft between the Cliffs of the depths of nearly 300 feet at least. This cleft is filled with trees & bushes in the narrow part; and as it widens becomes bare, if it were not for primroses on one side, which spread to the very verge of the Sea, and some fishermen's huts on the other, perched midway in the Ballustrades of beautiful green Hedges along their steps down to the sands.—But the sea, Jack, the sea—the little waterfall—then the white cliff—then St. Catherine's Hill—'the sheep in the meadows, the cows in the corn.'[6]

Keats continues his description, and then requests sketches of his brothers and of Reynolds. Professor Bate's analysis of Keats's mood at the time is significant:

. . . without transition, we turn from this thought of Tom, George, and Reynolds to his readiness to commit himself in this new endeavor, and its association with the Margate excursion when he had first seen the sea. With an attempted lightness of phrase, he says that 'From want of regular rest, I have been rather *narvus*—and the passage in Lear—"Do you not hear the sea?" has haunted me intensely.' And he

[6] *Ibid.,* 130–31.

copies out the fine sonnet 'On the Sea,' which he has just
written. The incident repeats the pattern started at Margate
and in a sense continued throughout his career. Preparing to
write a major poem, and not making the headway his time-
table demands, he writes a shorter one on the side—usually
an excellent one. Back in Margate he had broken the ice
with the sonnet 'To my Brother George,' the best part of
which dwells on the sea. Now, in his second Margate,
troubled further by the huge, uncertain grandeur of *King
Lear,* he writes another and much better sonnet, this time one
openly 'On the Sea.' The suggestions of promise, vastness,
uncertainties, again catch at him—the 'eternal whisperings,'
the mighty swell that gluts 'ten thousand caverns' [sic], the
thought of the *wideness* of the sea.[7]

It is important to notice that both storm and calm are moods
of the sea as it is described in the sonnet. But the sea's range of
mood, its very ambiguity, what Bate calls its "suggestions of
promise, vastness, uncertainties,"[8] can mollify one whose life
is engaged in getting and spending. As was the case with Cortez,
eyes are an important part of the sonnet.

Amy Lowell's comments on this poem are worth quoting because they establish again the ambiguity of the sea.

The sonnet is less a picture than a synthesis. Its added depth
and seriousness, its awareness of the ocean's vast, majestic
indifference, of the consolation offered by the view of this
resistless force and overwhelming elemental grandeur, show
how far Keats had moved since the year before, when he
was at Margate. Admirable as was his sea picture in the
sonnet *To My Brother George,* written there, cogent as were
its suggestions, it cannot be compared to this new sonnet, so
greatly does the last poem surpass the first.[9]

But, as we have seen, the earlier sonnet was far more than

---

[7] Bate, pp. 160–61. His italics.

[8] *Ibid.,* p. 160.

[9] Lowell, I, 305.

a seascape. Miss Lowell, in her eagerness to praise the later poem, in effect denies her insights into the earlier.

That the perception of the eternality and indifference of the sea became a source of consolation to Keats does not indicate a fatalistic outlook, but rather a mature acceptance of the conditions of human existence. The sea's power to console us by reasserting permanence, though not certainty, is found again in another sonnet, "When I have fears that I may cease to be." Keats's fears that a premature death will not allow him to trace the poetry he sees written

> upon the night's starr'd face,
> Huge cloudy symbols of a high romance,
> (lines 5–6)

his fears that an early death will not allow him to

> relish in the faery power
> Of unreflecting love,
> (lines 11–12)

are diminished by the sea. When he feels these fears,

> then on the shore
> Of the wide world I stand alone and think
> Till love and fame to nothingness do sink.[10]
> (lines 12–14)

---

[10] M. A. Goldberg has outlined the rhetorical movement of the sonnet and has pointed out that "By the close of the sonnet the protagonist has established a new scale of values, based no longer on an opposition between life and death forces, but instead on a contradistinction of Thing and Value. Thus, in the final line, when poetry and love 'to nothingness do sink,' thing has been subordinated to value, poetry and love have been subordinated to their essence, and the world of mortality has been left behind for the immutable, the fixed, the essential." "The Fears of John Keats," *MLQ,* XVIII (June 1957), 125–131. This quotation is taken from p. 129.

As has been noticed by Bate, Ward, and Blackstone,[11] the comfort usually provided by the sea was absent at the time of the composition of the epistle "To J. H. Reynolds," which contains the following passage:

> Dear Reynolds, I have a mysterious tale
> And cannot speak it. The first page I read
> Upon a Lampid rock of green sea weed
> Among the breakers—'Twas a quiet Eve;
> The rocks were silent—the wide sea did weave
> An untumultuous fringe of silver foam
> Along the flat brown sand. I was at home,
> And should have been most happy—but I saw
> Too far into the sea; where every maw
> The greater on the less feeds evermore:—
> But I saw too distinct into the core
> Of an eternal fierce destruction,
> And so from Happiness I far was gone.
>   (lines 86–98)

We know why he "should have been most happy," but we ought not be surprised that the sea is the source of "detested moods" (line 111). The significations of the symbol that produces the moods have generated one part of the amalgam of feeling that the sea has always provoked, and the idea of eternality is pervasive.

Eternality persists as the core of the relationship we are tracing in the sonnet "To Ailsa Rock," a mountain looming out of the sea. But it is not mere eternality that causes distress, rather it is the fear of eternal silence, obliteration from the memories of mankind.

> Hearken, thou craggy ocean pyramid!
> Give answer from thy voice, the sea-fowl's screams!
> When were thy shoulders mantled in huge streams?

---

[11] Bate, p. 309; Ward, p. 172; Blackstone, p. 153.

When from the sun was thy broad forehead hid?
How long is't since the mighty Power bid
    Thee heave to airy sleep from fathom dreams?
    Sleep in the lap of thunder or sunbeams,
Or when grey clouds are thy cold coverlid?
Thou answer'st not; for thou art dead asleep;
    Thy life is but two dead eternities—
The last in air, the former in the deep;
    First with the whales, last with the eagle-skies—
Drown'd wast thou till an earthquake made thee steep,
    Another cannot wake thy giant size.

Amy Lowell was reluctant to press the thematic connection between the sonnets we have been discussing:

> It is, perhaps, pushing possibilities somewhat far to suggest that the sonnet *To My Brother George,* written at Margate in 1816, and the sonnet *On the Sea,* written at Carisbrooke in 1817, have a certain thematic connection with *Ailsa Rock.* This is a point to be glanced at merely, nothing more.[12]

However, I think we have seen that the relationship is not so tenuous or so slight as all that. The possibilities inherent in the many significations of the sea as a symbol and as a stimulus to emotion have been thoroughly explored by Keats in the poems we have been discussing. The progress of his thought may be easily charted: he began with a perception of the totality and complexity of the sea, moved through stunned surprise at the sea's vastness of implication to a position where he could derive comfort from it. Then, having explored wideness, he discovered depth, and with it fear, and this became so related to the persistent recognition of the eternality of the sea that the symbol never again functioned in the early way. Keats moved from an ability to utilize ambiguity and tolerate ambivalence to the need to say either-or.

If we can extend the following statement by Perkins to

---

[12] Lowell, II, 43.

poems rather than poem, we can see this manipulation of symbol as typically Keatsian:

> The poet often appears in the poems not as a manipulator directing his symbols, or as a direct commentator, but in a dynamic and changing relation to the controlling symbols, reacting differently to them through the course of the poem as their fuller potential significance is gradually disclosed.[13]

Even in the "Bright Star" sonnet one can consider

> The moving waters at their priestlike task
> Of pure ablution round earth's human shores
> (lines 5–6)

to be inimical to the necessary warmth and passion of human love.[14] In this sonnet, as possibly in the sonnet "On the Sea," there is a loss of consciousness, but here there is death, not a dying into life: no sea nymphs quire, albeit the death is a luxurious one.

David Ormerod finds that the sea in the "Bright Star" sonnet is an "image of heaving flux." He compares the image of the star as Keats employs it in this sonnet with the "throbbing star" of the "Eve of St. Agnes" and, after examining some thematic similarities, concludes that the sonnet rejects the Christian ascetic spiritual approach to eternity in favor of "his own pagan and sensual approach, where body and soul are mingled and harmonized." Ormerod also states that the last line "envisages nothing less than an eternity of coitus—an embrace lasting forever, or, what comes to the same thing, recurrent swooning to death in the sexual climax."[15]

I cannot agree that the two alternatives come to the same

---

[13] Perkins, p. 196.

[14] Compare *Ibid.*, pp. 232–33.

[15] "Nature's Eremite: Keats and the Liturgy of Passion," *K-SJ*, XVI (1967), 74–75.

thing. The condition described from line nine through the
first half of line fourteen,

> No,—yet still steadfast, still unchangeable,
>   Pillow'd upon my fair love's ripening breast,
> To feel forever its soft fall and swell,
>   Awake forever in a sweet unrest,
> Still, still to hear her tender-taken breath,
> And so live ever,

seems to be the emotional equivalent of these lines from the
"Ode on a Grecian Urn":

> Bold Lover, never, never canst thou kiss,
> Though winning near the goal—yet, do not grieve;
>   She cannot fade, though thou hast not thy bliss,
>   For ever wilt thou love, and she be fair.
> . . .
> More happy love! more happy, happy love!
>   For ever warm and still to be enjoy'd,
>   For ever panting, and for ever young;
> All breathing human passion far above.
>   (lines 17–20, 25–28)

The alternative in the last half of line fourteen is to "swoon
to death," which may well be sexually luxurious but which is
not Keats's usual sort of dying into life—that is, a painful
transition from a state of ignorance to a state of enlightenment—but rather a dying into a world of flux, process, and
death.

[10]

The Nature of The Soil

Too few readers of Keats's poetry have been teased into thought by the minor poems. The major poetry is so much more aesthetically satisfying and philosophically mature than his other poetry that there may have seemed no reason to eat bread when we might have cake. Life is too short for us to spend much time explicating poor poetry. But neglect breeds contempt, with the result that existing comments or interpretations tend to become Authorized Versions. The danger in the case of Keats's poetry is not that we have ignored reading some overlooked masterpiece, but that we may be led into making false generalizations about the poetry as a whole. (Some such generalizations are examined in the first part of the appendix to this study.) The next two chapters demonstrate the importance to the canon of two unread Keats poems, "Specimen of an Induction to a Poem" and "Calidore."

Walter Jackson Bate calls "Specimen of an Induction to a Poem" a "fragment," and says it is but "sixty-eight lines of descriptive introduction to a tale" that never evolved. Bate doubts that it was intended "only as a preliminary exercise" because "this would have been unlike his usual practice." The structure of the poem, according to Bate, "falls roughly into two parts, the first of which consists of variations on the opening lines. . . ." He finds that "the images that cluster around his [Keats's] basic line—repeated once again ('Yet must I tell a tale of chivalry')—tend to be more vivid than the others: the line, significantly an expression of intention, may well have been the only specific detail he had in mind before he began." Because Bate's ideas about Keats and his poetry are likely to be considered standard, if not definitive, I shall quote his description of the remainder of the poem.

> Midway through the fragment it is plain that no tale is to come. The assertions begin to give way to the questionings, the self-doubt alternating with moments of hope or trust that create the main interest of "Sleep and Poetry" eight or nine months later: "Ah! shall I ever tell . . . No, no! this is far off. . . ." But then comes a suggestion of what, within less than two years, was to prove so unpredictably valuable— the trustful, imaginative approach to great writers of the past . . . that Longinus advocated. . . .[1]

Similarly Claude Finney says, "No doubt Keats desired to tell a tale of chivalry, but, unfortunately, he had only a picture in his mind."[2] Amy Lowell too finds the poem "a picture spoilt, and a story never begun," though she attributes this to Keats's attempting to do not what he could but what he thought he should.[3]

These comments are typical of the criticism and interpretation the poem has received, and it seems to me they are deficient on two counts: First, they assume that the poem is incomplete, taking the title to mean *a part of* rather than *an example of* an induction to a poem; second, they attribute the lack of a narrative line to a lack of planning or ability on Keats's part. I suggest that a closer examination of the poem, and a comparison to the sonnet "To Spenser"—which invokes the same poet as a source of inspiration—will show that a coherent, complete, lyrical statement is made in the poem, and that it is not entirely Keats's fault if a tale of chivalry is untold, not only in this poem but in others (especially "Calidore") as well.

---

[1] Bate, pp. 60–61.

[2] Finney, I, 103.

[3] Lowell, I, 127.

Lines 1–10 of the "Induction" make the statement that the speaker *"must* tell a tale of chivalry" (emphasis added), and describe the scene in his eye which impels him—a scene, Finney suggests, from "The Story of Rimini," by Hunt (Libertas). Lines 11–22, or two lines more than the opening statement whose structure they parallel, insist that the speaker "must tell a tale of chivalry" because another scene is present before him. This time the scene is populated with human beings, though they are scarcely actors: a lady with cold feet and a resting knight, both of whom are subordinate in interest to the lance that "points slantingly" or "rests" against a tree. The speaker asks, in lines 23–30, whether he shall ever tell a tale, either of the cruelty of the lance when it is wielded in battle or of the "grandeur of the balancing" when the knight with a spirit of "calm intent / Leaps to the honors of a tournament." The focus here is primarily on the knight and his emotions. Now a fifteen-line section tells us that these actions, these perceptions, these times of heroism and beauty are "far off." The problem is to resuscitate or "Revive the dying tones of minstrelsy." The sounds are not dead, though they are faint, and from them the speaker can revive fragments of the total picture, as he proceeds to do for eleven lines. That the tones are dying is no fault of the poet; he is given his environment and he could not have constructed it to be similar to the age of chivalry. But he does hear dying tones; he would like to penetrate that realm of visionary imagination whence the tones come, and the young Keats seems to feel that such a penetration is the function and the privilege of the poet. As in the epistle "To my Brother George," it is a chivalric scene the poet strains to see, and the introduction to the scene is by a tone or note that the poet is privileged to hear:

> When the bright warder blows his trumpet clear,
> Whose tones reach nought on earth but Poet's ear.
> When these enchanted portals open wide,
> And through the light the horsemen swiftly glide,

The Poet's eye can reach those golden halls,
And view the glory of their festivals.
(lines 31–36)

Byron's soul caught such a note, and the echo in the "Induction" from the earlier poem is interesting.

> Byron! how sweetly sad thy melody!
>   Attuning still the soul to tenderness,
>   As if soft Pity, with unusual stress,
> Had touch'd her plaintive lute, and thou, being by,
> Hadst caught the tones, nor suffered them to die.
("Sonnet to Byron," lines 1–5)

Another instance of these dying tones occurs in the "Ode to Apollo," which is, as Walter Evert has convincingly demonstrated, a crucial poem for an understanding of Keats's aesthetic theory. The ode describes how

> Bards, that erst sublimely told
>   Heoric deeds, and sang of fate,
> With fervour seize their adamantine lyres.
(lines 3–5)

But Spenser, in the sixth stanza, plays no stringed instrument, lyre or lute:

> A silver trumpet Spenser blows,
>   And, as its martial notes to silence flee,
> From a virgin chorus flows
>   A hymn in praise of spotless Chastity.
(lines 30–33)

Then Keats seems to have remembered the family of instruments he began with, for

> 'Tis still! Wild warblings from the Aeolian lyre
> Enchantment softly breathe, and tremblingly expire.
(lines 34–35)

The poem ends when Apollo

> joinest with the Nine,
> And all the powers of song combine,
>   We listen here on earth :[4]
> The dying tones that fill the air,
> And charm the ear of evening fair,
> From thee, great God of Bards, receive their heavenly birth.
>   (lines 43–47)

The importance of these comparisons is that they establish the faintness of the trumpet-call of inspiration, they assert that the sensitive ear of the true poet is needed to hear it, to derive inspiration from it, and to be led by it into (or back into) an age or a land of chivalry and romance. There can be little doubt that the land that lies beyond "enchanted portals" is not immediately present.

At line 45 of the "Induction" the speaker once again, and for the last time, sees a picture—a mighty steed and a gentle, though proud knight—and once again the fit is upon him : "Yet must I tell a tale of chivalry." But notice the difference here. No longer is there an opening "Lo!"; now the imperativeness is much more strongly stressed. Alas, the image of the steed and its rider lasts only three lines. At that point, at line 49, the speaker begins a prayer to Spenser. We are made aware that it is a prayer addressed to one disposed to grant prayers, one who has provided not only pleasure to the speaker but inspiration to his friend Libertas. Therefore, though aware of his "daring" and "strange pretence," the speaker feels confident that the generosity of the Bard (Spenser), his own sense of meekness and "due reverence," and the attestation of Hunt give him cause to "hope" to see the enchanted realm.

So we have a complete poem, one that sets forth what is re-

---

4 Similarly, Chatterton's voice "Melted in dying numbers" (line 6), and in "Endymion," I, 141–44 we learn of shepherds who

> Sat listening round Apollo's pipe,
> When the great deity, for earth too ripe,
> Let his divinity o'er-flowing die
> In music.

quired of the poet, the sort of inspiration he needs, the lack of this inspiration in the present environment, and the result of the conjunction of proper poet with proper environment and inspiration. The "Induction" is a poem that prays for such a favorable conjunction for the suppliant, who vigorously desires to enter and recapture completely, not just in fragments, an enchanted realm of chivalry and romance.

The sonnet "To Spenser" deals with similar materials and uses similar relationships expressed in familiar diction. It was written two years after "Induction," but by now it should be no surprise to find early configurations of themes and relationships reappearing in poetry written later in Keats's career. In the "Induction" the speaker expresses some fear that Spenser will

> Be jealous that the foot of other wight
> Should madly follow that bright path of light
> Trac'd by thy lov'd Libertas;
>> (lines 59–61)

but he hastens to assure Spencer that he follows not madly but with "due reverence," and that Libertas will attest to that. In the sonnet, it is the speaker who is jealous of Spenser, though jealous in a particular way. He would like to be able to "refine / Some English that might strive thine ear to please," but he explains that he cannot create what might be a "bright path of light"[5] because his environment prohibits it. He is "an inhabitant of the wintry earth" (line 6) who cannot "Rise, like Phoebus . . . / Fire-Wing'd" (lines 7–8).

> It is impossible to escape from toil
>> O' the sudden, and receive thy spiriting:

---

[5] The poetry of A.G.S. is also called a "brightening path" which the muse might resent Keats's "assaying."

> The flower must drink the nature of the soil
> Before it can put forth its blossoming
>   (lines 9–12)

This tells us that the environment of the poet, the "wintry earth," has frozen "the nature," the vivifying power, and so the poet can draw no sustenance, no inspiration from his surroundings. As in "The Fall of Hyperion" he must wait for the time

> When in mid-May the sickening East-wind
> Shifts sudden to the South, the small warm rain
> Melts out the frozen incense from all flowers.
>   (lines 97–99)[6]

Approximately two weeks earlier Keats had thought of Spenser in conjunction with a lute and with winter, but then he bade him away:

> O golden-tongued Romance with serene lute!
> Fair plumed Syren, Queen of far away!
> Leave melodizing on this wintry day,
> Shut up thine olden pages, and be mute.
>   ("On Sitting Down to Read
>   *King Lear* Once Again,"
>   lines 1–4)

(DeSelincourt points out that winter and Spenser are associated in both sonnets, but he makes nothing of it. p. 544) In this sonnet Keats hopes that he will not be allowed to "wander in a barren dream" (line 12). This represents a rejection of the realm of visionary imagination for that of reality.

Two weeks after the sonnet "To Spenser" the familiar relationship was expressed again, this time in the unrhymed sonnet

---

[6] This idea can be found at least once in the letters. Writing on 14 February to the George Keatses he says: "I have not gone on with Hyperion—for to tell the truth I have not been in great cue for writing lately—I must wait for the sp[r]ing to rouse me up a little." (*Letters,* II, 62).

"What the Thrush Said." The bird promises that he who has suffered during winter will be granted a rich spring, that he who has suffered and struggled in the darkness will have a trebly bright morn. The thrush advises—much as the nightingale might have advised:

> O fret not after knowledge—I have none,
> And yet my song comes native with the warmth.[7]
>
> (lines 9–10)

That is, penetration into the enchanted realm is possible. It will come without strain or force, in good time, nearly as naturally as leaves to a tree, as good poetry should.

It seems then that these poems confirm the brief statement in "Induction," especially in lines 31–33, that it is not the poet alone who is at fault. The tones of minstrelsy are dying, melodies heard from or announcing an enchanted land or age penetrable by the imagination are growing faint; they do not provide the clarion inspiration they did when both knighthood and poetry were in flower. It is not wholly that the poet lacks the ability to tell a tale of chivalry, though, as I have pointed out, some—like Byron—can do much with dying tones, but it is also that no such tasks are currently available, none are part of the poet's environment.[8] The "Induction" is, largely, a prayer that the poet be helped by Spenser into the realm of the imagination because reality cannot provide the grail for which he quests. The poem is a complete, successful, and very early statement of a theme whose alternatives constantly tantalized and tormented Keats, and found expression in much of his best poetry.

---

[7] See Chapter 6, on knowledge, and Ward, pp. 166–67, who does not see the link with production.

[8] Keats makes use of this theme in at least one poem, "Robin Hood," where he laments that commerce has destroyed the pleasant world Robin and his band knew. Despite this, Keats says, we can sing in honor of them. In this poem, too, emphasis is placed on the wintry landscape and, if not dying, dead tones.

[11]

Was There a Poet Born?

Perhaps few would argue against the deprecation that has been heaped on "Calidore." However, it must be read, if only for the reason Amy Lowell gives: "no one who has not read it can appreciate what Keats had to outgrow."[1] Of course her judgment does not preclude criticism or analysis, though it contains enough truth to forestall it. That no one has yet commented on the underlying story, the growth of the poet, is not surprising.

In a famous passage in "Sleep and Poetry," which has reminded almost every critic of a parallel description of the maturation process in "Tintern Abbey," Keats asks for

> ten years, that I may overwhelm
> Myself in poesy; so I may do the deed
> That my own soul has to itself decreed.
> Then will I pass the countries that I see
> In long perspective, and continually
> Taste their pure fountains. First the realm I'll pass
> Of Flora, and old Pan: sleep in the grass,
> Feed upon apples red, and strawberries,
> And choose each pleasure that my fancy sees;

---

[1] Lowell, I, 130.

Catch the white-handed nymphs in shady places,
To woo sweet kisses from averted faces,—
Play with their fingers, touch their shoulders white
Into a pretty shrinking with a bite
As hard as lips can make it: till agreed,
A lovely tale of human life we'll read.
And one will teach a tame dove how it best
May fan the cool air gently o'er my rest;
Another, bending o'er her nimble tread,
Will set a green robe floating round her head,
And still will dance with ever varied ease,
Smiling upon the flowers and the trees:
Another will entice me on, and on
Through almond blossoms and rich cinnamon;
Till in the bosom of a leafy world
We rest in silence, like two gems upcurl'd
In the recesses of a pearly shell.

And can I ever bid these joys farewell?
Yes, I must pass them for a nobler life,
Where I may find the agonies, the strife
Of human hearts.

(lines 96–125)

The same organic process can be detected in "Calidore." The first fifty-four lines are given to cataloguing "the realm / Of Flora, and old Pan," supposedly intimately known by our eponymous hero. But, as Amy Lowell points out, "There could hardly be a greater number of factual errors, all contained in a few lines, than there are in this passage."[2] However, we can suppose that Keats was unaware of this, and that achieving a lush sensuousness was more important than fidelity to fact. Or we could say that Calidore would have become as faulty a nature poet as "Calidore" is a narrative romance. Yet the underlying story is essentially unchanged. At any rate, Calidore delights in nature. He does not

---

[2] *Ibid.,* 128.

> pass lightly by
> Objects that look'd out so invitingly
> On either side. These, gentle Calidore
> Greeted, as he had known them long before.
>   (lines 30–33)

Calidore's catalogue of blisses is spared any more inaccuracies by a highly significant interruption:

> his glad senses caught
> A trumpet's silver voice. Ah! it was fraught
> With many joys for him: the warder's ken
> Had found white coursers prancing in the glen.

Such music, as we have seen before, is a signal that the realm of the visionary imagination is in our purview. But it is not brought into the poem at this point. If one had sufficient temerity one could argue that the failure to discuss the highest realm of poetry is as planned as it is appropriate: the highest realm cannot be discussed now because Calidore has not yet passed through the second stage of growth, he has yet to read a lovely tale of human life. This he does while assisting the ladies from their palfreys.

> what a kiss,
> What gentle squeeze he gave each lady's hand!
> How tremblingly their delicate ankles spann'd!
> Into how sweet a trance his soul was gone,
> While whisperings of affection
> Made him delay to let their tender feet
> Come to the earth; with an incline so sweet
> From their low palfreys o'er his neck they bent:
> And whether there were tears of languishment,
> Or that the evening dew had pearl'd their tresses,
> He feels a moisture on his cheek, and blesses
> With lips that tremble, and with glistening eye
> All the soft luxury
> That nestled in his arms. A dimpled hand,
> Fair as some wonder out of fairy land,

Hung from his shoulder like the drooping flowers
Of whitest Cassia, fresh from summer showers:
And this he fondled with his happy cheek
As if for joy he would no further seek.
                    (lines 80–98)

Movement toward the next stage begins to be suggested at
this point in the poem. We are already familiar with the
Keatsian proto-poet standing on a promontory contemplating
poetry and eternity. In Calidore we are given our first glimpse
of him.

      The kind voice of good Sir Clerimond
    Came to his ear, like something from beyond
    His present being: so he gently drew
    His warm arms, thrilling now with pulses new,
    From their sweet thrall, and forward gently bending,
    Thank'd heaven that his joy was never ending;
    While 'gainst his forehead he devoutly press'd
    A hand heaven made to succor the distress'd;
    A hand that from the world's bleak promontory
    Had lifted Calidore for deeds of glory.
                    (lines 99–108)

The notion of relieving the distressed as it achieves expression in this context associates this poet *soi-disant* far more
closely with the poet kings of "Sleep and Poetry," "who simply
tell the most heart-easing things" (line 268), than with the
humanist-physician of "The Fall of Hyperion."

After this, Sir Clerimond introduces Calidore to Sir Gondibert, whose example presumably will elevate Calidore to aspire
to knightly or poetic greatness.

      Amid the pages, and the torches' glare,
    There stood a knight, patting the flowing hair
    Of his proud horse's mane: he was withal
    A man of elegance, and stature tall:

So that the waving of his plumes would be
High as the berries of a wild ash tree,
Or as the winged cap of Mercury.
His armour was so dexterously wrought
In shape, that sure no living man had thought
It hard, and heavy steel: but that indeed
It was some glorious form, some splendid weed,
In which a spirit new come from the skies
Might live, and show itself to human eyes.
'Tis the far-fam'd, the brave Sir Gondibert,
Said the good man to Calidore alert;
While the young warrior with a step of grace
Came up,—a courtly smile upon his face,
And mailed hand held out, ready to greet
The large-eyed wonder, and ambitious heat
Of the aspiring boy; who as he led
Those smiling ladies, often turned his head
To admire the visor arched so gracefully
Over a knightly brow.
                              (lines 109–131)

In the "Induction" Spenser is described much as Gondibert is:

Yet must I tell a tale of chivalry:
Or wherefore comes that steed so proudly by?
Wherefore more proudly does the gentle knight
Rein in the swelling of his ample might?
Spenser! thy brows are arched, open, kind.
                              (lines 45–49)

But Calidore is not yet ready to be elevated to poet or knight-hood, for he is unwilling to depart from the second stage of growth.

              young Calidore is burning
To hear of knightly deeds, and gallant spurning
Of all unworthiness; and how the strong of arm
Kept off dismay, and terror, and alarm

> From lovely woman: while brimful of this
> He gave each damsel's hand so warm a kiss,
> And had such manly ardour in his eye,
> That each at other look'd half staringly.
>   (lines 142–149)

There is some lapse of time and a significant change of focus between the conclusions of the above description and the concluding lines of the poem. Perhaps Keats knew a pause was needed here, for the final lines present the familiar collocation of elements indigenous to the realm of the visionary imagination where the highest form of poetry might be composed.

> Softly the breezes from the forest came,
> Softly they blew aside the taper's flame;
> Clear was the song from Philomel's far bower;
> Grateful the incense from the lime-tree flower;
> Mysterious, wild, the far heard trumpet's tone;
> Lovely the moon in ether, all alone:
> Sweet too the converse of these happy mortals,
> As that of busy spirits when the portals
> Are closing in the west; or that soft humming
> We hear around when Hesperus is coming.
> Sweet be their sleep.
>   (lines 152–62)

Most of these elements can be found in the "Ode to a Nightingale":[3] incense, breezes altering the patterns of light and dark, specific reference to the moon, the song of a nightingale in a bower or plot of green. Earlier in "Calidore" we learned of

> Delicious sounds! those little bright-eyed things
> That float about the air on azure wings,
>   (lines 73–74)

---

[3] As E. C. Pettet has shown, though to no thematic point, in his second chapter.

but then they were "less heartfelt" by Calidore than the "clang of horses hoofs," even as he was "Deaf to the nightingale's first under-song" (line 61). The lines on the delicious sounds adumbrate a line in the nightingale ode: "The murmurous haunt of flies on summer eves" (line 50).

The other elements, the trumpet's tone, the portals closing in the west, and so on, are familiar parts of Keats's conceptual view of art as described by Walter Evert.[4] It is not without significance or poignancy that the poem breaks off where it does. Neither Calidore nor Keats was yet a poet. Although the spiritual environment was ripe, the bachelor was not.

Because of the concatenation of conceptual elements, the "busy spirits" referred to in line 159 of "Calidore" are likely to be bards of passion and mirth, or "Souls of poets dead and gone." The sweet conversations of the happy mortals are, then, like those of poets. More likely, they are actually poetry. Friendship and conversation and poetry are part of a relationship that has been discussed by J. Middleton Murry, whose rhapsodic discussion of "Keats and Friendship" makes some points about the relationship between friendship and poetry that are not substantiated by the relationships discoverable in Keats's poetry. Murry finds that while on the road to discovering "the beauty of the whole truth"[5]

> . . . Keats never left his hold of his admiration for simple moral beauty. He deliberately preferred it to genius, if there had to be a choice between them.

> 'So I do believe (he wrote to his brothers on January 13th, 1818)—not thus speaking with any poor vanity—that works of genius are the first things in this world. No! for that sort of probity and disinterestedness which such

---

[4] Evert, p. 59, includes "Calidore" in tracing key imaginal clusters.

[5] Murry, p. 307.

men as Bailey possess does hold and grasp the tiptop of any spiritual honors that can be payed to anything in this world. And moreover having this feeling come over me in its full force, I sat down to write you with a grateful heart, in that I had not a brother who did not feel and credit me for a deeper feeling and devotion for his uprightness, than for any marks of genius however splendid.'

There, evidently, speaks the inmost self of Keats. And this integrity, or moral beauty, is for Keats, the condition of friendship. Friendship is the mutual response to this quality. Hence his admiration for Georgiana Wylie, his brother George's wife. 'I like her better and better—she is the most disinterested woman I ever knew.' And that is why, in the extempore acrostic he wrote on her name, he declared his faith again that loyalty in friendship was as noble and indeed divine as supreme poetic achievement: they equally belonged to the order of ultimate reality.

> Imagine not that greatest mastery
> And Kingdom over all the Realms of verse
> Nears more to Heaven in aught than when we *nurse*
> And surety give to love and Brotherhood.
>   (Italics added)

But there lies behind this a process more elemental and less philosophical than Murry detects. In his early sonnet "To Solitude" Keats says he would gladly trace scenes of natural beauty with solitude,

> Yet the sweet converse of an innocent mind,
>   Whose words are images of thoughts refin'd,
> Is my soul's pleasure; and it sure must be
>   Almost the highest bliss of human-kind,
> When to thy haunts two kindred spirits flee.
>   (lines 11–14)

These haunts are, of course, "places of nestling green for

poets made" in which Keats typically creates or thinks of creating poetry. Words which are images of thoughts refined (depending on the connotation of refined—the chemical is best) is an adequate definition of poetry.

"For Sweet Relief" from thoughts of the immensity of the poet's task as outlined in "Sleep and Poetry" Keats says,

> I'll dwell
> On humbler thoughts, and let this strange assay
> Begun in gentleness die so away.
> E'en now all tumult from my bosom fades:
> I turn full hearted to the friendly aids
> That smooth the path of honour; brotherhood,
> And friendliness the *nurse* of mutual good.
> The hearty grasp that sends a pleasant sonnet
> Into the brain ere one can think upon it.
>   (lines 312–20, Italics added)

Thus we can see that friendship and poetry not only belong to the same order of reality, not only are the negatively capable qualities of personality necessary for both, but both are wrought at the same instant out of the same process.

[12]

Secrets of Some Wond'rous Thing

The history and authenticity of the sonnet "The Poet" have been examined and questioned extensively, but there is not, as far as I can tell, any determination that can be regarded as final. The debate seems to have trickled to an end, Bernard Blackstone's plea for "further information" and "present consensus of opinion" having been ignored since its publication in 1958.[1] Complicating the problem are two versions of the poem, one in the *London Magazine* of October, 1821, the other in the Morgan Library's Woodhouse book. Amy Lowell's unfortunate mistranscription of the latter[2] is an additional frustration.

Earl Wasserman's rejoinder[3] to Elmer Brooks' article on "The Poet," especially the *London Magazine* version,[4] argues that the Woodhouse version is very likely attributable to Keats: "it is difficult to doubt his authorship."[5] Wasserman's evidence consists primarily of a number of parallels in matter and manner between "The Poet" and "Endymion." Mabel Steele's argument[6] that neither version is Keats's is weakened, it seems to me,

---

1 *Times Literary Supplement,* 13 Nov. 1959, 661.

2 Elmer Brooks, " 'The Poet' An Error in the Keats canon?" *MLN,* LXVII (Nov. 1952), 453.

3 "Keats' sonnet 'The Poet,' " *MLN,* LXVII (Nov. 1952), 454–56.

4 Brooks, pp. 450–54.

5 Wasserman, p. 454.

6 "The Authorship of 'The Poet' and other Sonnets," *K-SJ,* V (1956), 69–80.

by its nearly total dependence on Hessey's copy of *A Collection of English Sonnets* by R. F. Housman. Miss Steele argues that Wasserman assumes too much by suggesting that the poem was written some time before its publication.[7] However, she does not account for the note in the Woodhouse book which says that the sonnet was written "About 1815/6."[8] In H. W. Garrod's preface to the second edition of *The Poetical Works of John Keats* (Oxford, 1958), he comments that Miss Steele "*may* be right [his italics]," (p. vii).

If I may proceed one step further on this dangerous terrain, I should like to present two arguments about the date of the poem, both of which are favorable to the sort of investigation I shall make as soon as this bibliographical jungle is mapped. Harold Briggs dates "The Poet" December, 1816, and in his chronology this makes the sonnet contemporaneous with "Sleep and Poetry."[9] Amy Lowell suggests August-September, 1816 as the probable time of composition, a time shortly before the beginning of Keats's work on "Sleep and Poetry."[10]

Now let us look at the best text of the best version of "The Poet."

> At morn, at noon, at Eve, and Middle Night
>   He passes forth into the charmed air,
>   With talisman to call up spirits rare
> From plant, cave, rock, and fountain.—To his sight
> The husk of natural objects opens quite
>   To the core: and every secret essence there
>   Reveals the elements of good and fair;
> Making him see, where Learning hath no light.
> Sometimes above the gross and palpable things
>   Of this diurnal sphere, his spirit flies
>   On awful wing; and with its destined skies

---

[7] Steele, p. 74.

[8] Lowell, I, 163.

[9] *The Complete Poetry and Selected Prose of John Keats* (New York, 1951), vi–vii.

[10] Lowell, I, 165.

Holds premature and mystic communings:
Till such unearthly intercourses shed
A visible halo round his mortal head.[11]

Wasserman has shown many relationships between the ideas in "The Poet" and those in "Endymion," and in small part, to those in "Sleep and Poetry," though to the latter only to explain a phrase in the less Keatsian version. He shows that the sonnet concerns fellowship with essence by means of negative capability, and entrance into the "heavenly bourne," or the enchanted realm of the visionary imagination.[12] Blackstone similarly finds the poem to be "a precise statement of the poetic function," and he believes "we must suppose that Keats is speaking of himself, as he is or as he aspires to be."[13] Blackstone discovers a poet in the Hermetic tradition, a poet-magus who sees correspondences in a three-fold world, elementary, celestial, and intellectual; a poet interested in "ideas of mutual penetration, cyclic movement, transmutation, and sensible and ethereal elements."[14] "The purpose of the poet's passing forth," according to Blackstone, "is nothing less than the evocation of 'spirits' . . . those hypostasized [sic] expressions of the *Anima Mundi* which exists in plant, cave, rock, and fountain."[15]

I have no wish to quarrel with Wasserman's interpretation, nor with the essential part of Blackstone's. I hope to demonstrate that there is sufficient internal evidence of authenticity in this poem to justify Garrod's retention of it in his second edition.[16] It can be related as easily to a poem composed at nearly the same time, "Sleep and Poetry," as it can to "Endymion," composed six months to a year later.

---

[11] *The Poetical Works of John Keats,* ed. H. W. Garrod, 2nd ed., p. 528.

[12] Wasserman, extracted from pp. 454–56.

[13] Blackstone, p. 76.

[14] *Ibid.,* p. 78.

[15] *Ibid.,* p. 88.

[16] Garrod says in the preface to the second edition (p. vii), "Miss Steele *may* be right, but I would like the student of Keats to have the poem before him."

One of the things "Sleep and Poetry" provides us with, according to Blackstone, is a charioteer who does four things: "He descends from heaven; he 'talks to trees and mountains'; he summons a host of spirits; and he writes something down." Blackstone recognizes that "Once again, recognizably, we are in the world of 'The Poet'," but he does not elaborate.[17]

In "Sleep and Poetry" a charioteer—apparently Apollo or an archetypal poet—glides down to an earth whose environment has more in common with the "charmed air" of "The Poet" than with the "muddy stream" of "real things" in "Sleep and Poetry" (lines 157–58). This muddy stream corresponds to the "gross and palpable things / Of this diurnal sphere," which (similarly) are escaped from in the sonnet. The "charmed air" corresponds to lines 29–31 in "Sleep and Poetry" where we learn that Poetry sometimes comes

> like a gentle whispering
> Of all the secrets of some wond'rous thing
> That breathes about us in the vacant air.

The charioteer descends to a "green-Hill's side" (line 134) and talks with "trees and mountains" (line 137). By means of a "wond'rous gesture" (line 136), which is an analogue for the poet's "talisman," he "calls up spirits rare," "Shapes of delight, of mystery and fear" (line 138) to whom he seems to listen intently and whose wisdom he "writes with such a hurrying glow" (line 154). The potential denizen of the "wide heaven"

---

17 Blackstone, p. 107. Werner Beyer says "The imagery of *The Poet* also confirms our suggestion as to the identity of The Charioteer . . . in *Sleep and Poetry*" (p. 96), i.e., the daemon king, but he does not discuss the textural similarities other than attributing the imagery of both to his usual source. His book, in general, differs from my investigation in that Professor Beyer is far more interested in derivation than in expressive function. Pettet argues against neo-platonic interpretations saying; ". . . there is no reason to read anything specifically metaphysical into the opening lines which closely resemble the charioteer (The Spirit of Poetry and Imagination) in *Sleep and Poetry*" (p. 368).

of poesy is no less sure that if he were found worthy he would
have a vision of a "bowery nook" where he

> may copy many a lovely saying
> About the leaves, and flowers,—about the playing
> Of nymphs in woods, and fountains.
>
> (lines 64–66)

Later this too luxurious picture is modified, and the potential
poet imagines

> a spot
> Of awfuller shade, or an enchanted grot,
> Or a green-hill o'erspread with chequered dress
> Of flowers, and fearful from its lovliness,

(where he will)

> Write on my tablets all that was permitted,
> All that was for our human senses fitted.
> Then the events of this wide world I'd seize
> Like a strong giant, and my spirit teaze
> Till at its shoulders it should proudly see
> Wings to find out an immortality.
>
> (lines 75–84)

That is, his spirit, like that described in "The Poet," will fly
"on awful wing" and penetrate the realm of the visionary imagination. There will be a "visible halo" too, as a sign of achievement, though it will not be granted during life. The would-be
poet quite early has a glimpse of

> the laurel wreath on high suspended,
> That is to crown our name when life is ended.[18]
>
> (lines 35–36)

---

[18] For its relevance to the problems of dating, laurel crowns as visible
wreaths were on Keats's mind from November, 1816, when a young
lady sent him a crown which he commemorated in a sonnet, to
February, 1817, which is a likely date for the occasion at Hunt's
when he and Keats exchanged laurel wreaths.

The poet in "The Poet" is taught by the essences he has called forth; he is made to see "where Learning hath no light." Similarly, the potential poet in "Sleep and Poetry" says:

> though I am not wealthy in the dower
> Of spanning wisdom; though I do not know
> The shiftings of the mighty winds that blow
> Hither and thither all the changing thoughts
> Of man: though no great minist'ring reason sorts
> Out the dark mysteries of human souls
> To clear conceiving: yet there ever rolls
> A vast idea before me, and I glean
> Therefrom my liberty.

(lines 284–92)

Just as, in Brooks' words, "Surmise and circumstantial evidence can not outweigh Woodhouse's indication that Keats is the author of 'The Poet'," neither can numerous parallels of this sort prove it. Nevertheless I think it valuable to point out these parallels so that both sides in the debate—if there still is one going on—can be at full strength.

[13]

The Pleasures of Memory

Walter Evert, in tracing "significant extensions of the symbolism attached to Keats's central hypothesis,"[1] makes the following observation:

> One of these, which occurs frequently in Keats's poetry, is wine. The Poet's delight in good claret is a matter of record, and many of the references to wine in his poetry simply communicate the pleasure of drinking it. But there is also an occasional note of its utility as an intoxicant, an available Lethe, for the banishment of insistent memory. Such is its use in one of the earliest poems, 'Fill for me a brimming bowl,' in which the poet calls for it as an aid (which proves to be ineffectual) in the eradication of desire for a beautiful woman whom he affects to have seen. In one of his last poems, 'What can I do to drive away / Remembrance from my eyes?' which reflects his feelings about Fanny Brawne and strikingly resembles in development the earlier poem, he again meditates this easy way out, but rejects it as 'vulgarism.' In both cases the wine is literally intended, its function is negative, and it is rejected, in the former case as impractical, in the latter as improper.[2]

Sidney Colvin detects another poem that recalls the early

---

[1] Evert, p. 67.
[2] *Ibid.*, pp. 67–68.

effort. Of "Time's Sea Hath Been Five Years at Its Slow Ebb"
(or "To a Lady Seen for a Few Moments at Vauxhall") Colvin
remarks:

> But what is singular is that in the third quatrain should be
> recalled, in the same high strain of emotion, the vision of a
> beauty seen but not even accosted three-and-a-half years
> earlier (not really five) in the public gardens at Vauxhall,
> and then . . . addressed in what are almost the earliest of
> Keats's dated verses, those in which he calls for a 'brimming
> bowl.' . . . Such, Woodhouse assures us, is the case, and the
> same memory fills the second sonnet ["Time's Sea"].[3]

What seems to me even more singular is that these three
poems on the pleasures of memory exhibit so many other relationships not yet publicly noticed. It is most convenient to begin
developing the relationships with the earliest poem.

> Fill for me a brimming bowl
> And let me in it drown my soul:
> But put therein some drug, designed
> To Banish Women from my mind:
> For I want not the stream inspiring
> That fills the mind with fond desiring,
> But I want as deep a draught
> As ere from Lethe's wave was quaff'd;
> From my despairing heart to charm
> The image of the fairest form
> That e'er my reveling eyes beheld,
> That e'er my wandering fancy spell'd
> In vain! Away I cannot chace
> The melting softness of that face,
> The beaminess of those bright eyes,
> That breast—earth's only Paradise.
> My sight will never more be blest;
> For all I see has lost its zest:
> Nor with delight can I explore
> The Classic page, or Muse's lore.

---

[3] Colvin, p. 259.

Had she but known how beat my heart,
And with one smile reliev'd its smart,
I should have felt a sweet relief,
I should have felt 'the joy of grief.'
Yet as a Tuscan mid the snow
Of Lapland thinks on sweet Arno,
Even so for ever shall she be
The Halo of my Memory.

The poem to which this bears the most obvious resemblance is
"What can I do to drive away" (sometimes called "Lines to
Fanny," the "Second Ode to Fanny Brawne," or "To [Fanny]."
It is easily seen how this poem elaborates in concrete detail the
abstraction of the early poem.

What can I do to drive away
Remembrance from my eyes? For they have seen,
Aye, an hour ago, my brilliant Queen!
Touch has a memory. O say, love, say,
What can I do to kill it and be free
In my old liberty?
When every fair one that I saw was fair,
Enough to catch me in but half a snare,
Not keep me there:
When, howe'er poor or particolour'd things,
My muse had wings,
And ever ready was to take her course
Whither I bent her force,
Unintellectual, yet divine to me;—
Divine, I say!—what sea-bird o'er the sea
Is a philosopher the while he goes
Winging along where the great water throes?

How shall I do
To get anew
Those moulted feathers, and so mount once more
Above, above
The reach of fluttering Love,
And make him cower lowly while I soar?

Shall I gulp wine? No, that is vulgarism,
A heresy and schism,
Foisted into the cannon-law of love;—
No,—wine is only sweet to happy men;
More dismal cares
Seize on me unawares,—
Where shall I learn to get my peace again?
To banish thoughts of that most hateful land,
Dungeoner of my friends, that wicked strand
Where they were wreck'd and live a wrecked life;
That monstrous region, whose dull rivers pour,
Ever from their sordid urns unto the shore,
Unown'd of any weedy-haired gods;
Whose winds, all zephyrless, hold scourging rods,
Iced in the great lakes, to afflict mankind;
Whose rank-grown forests, frosted, black, and blind,
Would fright a Dryad; whose harsh herbag'd meads
Make lean and lank the starv'd ox while he feeds;
There bad flowers have no scent, birds no sweet song,
And great unerring Nature once seems wrong.

O, for some sunny spell
To dissipate the shadows of this hell!
Say they are gone,—with the new dawning light
Steps forth my lady bright!
O, let me once more rest
My soul upon that dazzling breast!
Let once again these aching arms be plac'd,
The tender gaolers of thy waist!
And let me feel that warm breath here and there
To spread a rapture in my very hair,—
O, the sweetness of the pain!
Give me those lips again!

Enough! Enough! it is enough for me
To dream of thee!

The ostensible problem in the two poems is the same: to
forget an image which is to some degree fairer or more powerful than those he has encountered before. Presumably one

method of forgetting, drinking, has proved efficacious previously, but this is no longer the case. In the early poem we learn that alcohol is no longer strong enough to provide the forgetfulness only seemingly sought for—indeed it appears that laudanum would not be effective against so powerful a memory. The poem goes on to suggest that even a smile from the woman would have allowed him to feel the " 'joy of grief'," which, though in juvenile and self-conscious form, is essentially of the order of perception attained in the final stanza of the "Ode on Melancholy."

> She dwells with Beauty—Beauty that must die;
> And Joy, whose hand is ever at his lips
> Bidding adieu; and aching pleasure nigh,
> Turning to poison while the bee-mouth sips:
> Ay, in the very temple of Delight
> Veil'd Melancholy has her sovran shrine.
> (lines 21–26)

In the ode "To [Fanny]" we find another expression of the same idea: even the memory of the "lady bright" is sufficient to provoke "the sweetness of the pain."

The feeling is similar to that he describes to Fanny on 1 July 1819:

I have never known any unalloy'd Happiness for many days together: the death or sickness of someone has always spoilt my hours—and now when none such troubles oppress me, it is you must confess very hard that another sort of pain should haunt me. Ask yourself my love whether you are not very cruel to have so entrammeled me, so destroyed my freedom. Will you confess this in the Letter you must write immediately and do all you can to console me in it—make it rich as a draught of poppies to intoxicate me—write the softest words and kiss them that I may at least touch my lips where yours have been.[4]

---

[4] *Letters,* II, 123.

Here we notice again memory and intoxication and the familiar pleasure-pain complex.[5]

If resting his "soul upon that dazzling breast" results when the shadows of his hellish thoughts are dissipated, then, much as in the earlier poem, "that breast—[is] earth's only Paradise." Probably Lapland seems every bit as barren to the Tuscan as America to Keats, and it ought to be mentioned that the Arno is a sweet not a dull river.

The ode exhibits another familiar relationship that needs to be examined at this time. It is evident in the ode that love has imprisoned Keats's muse, has tethered his fancy. His fancy was unintellectual and unphilosophical, but powerful and free. In the second stanza we learn that the speaker wants his unintellectual and unphilosophical fancy to mount lawfully "above / The reach of fluttering Love." Wine is not permitted; there can be no drunken drivers in love's realm.[6] There are suggestions that

---

[5] Professor E. C. Pettet has described the biographical significance of the ideas expressed in the ode "To Fanny" and the letters, though he does not discuss the same poems. He writes,

> All through his short life—it was one of his chief and most characteristic feelings—Keats was obsessed by the close juxtaposition of joy and grief, delight and pain. Nothing can have done more to intensify this obsession than his experience of love, and here in one of his last poems no sooner has he confessed his dream of sensuous delight than the old paradox bursts from him—
> O, the sweetness of the pain!
> Three months or so later . . . we find him writing to Fanny of 'The Love which has so long been my pleasure and my torment.'
> Into that sentence is compressed the true nature of the love he had experienced. Probably in his day to day life as the lover of Fanny Brawne—that life that had a crucial bearing on his love-poetry but was not identical with it—the pleasure and the torment approximately balanced. But in his poetry after the day-dream of *Endymion,* it was the torment that predominated. p. 250.

[6] See ch. 4, note 1, p. 66, for Professor Wasserman's comment on the rejection of wine. See also the rejection of the wine of earthly manufacture for Apollo's metaphoric brew in "Hence, Burgundy, Claret, and port!"

love and philosophy[7] are identified in this poem. Both are inimical to the kind of poetry he claims to have been writing:
love moulted his feathers much as philosophy would have
ballasted his wings, reduced his buoyancy. Only a month earlier,
on 19 March 1819, he had written to the George Keatses that
energy "is the very thing in which consists poetry; and if so it
is not so fine a thing as philosophy—For the same reason that
an eagle is not so fine a thing as a truth" (*Letters,* II, 80–81).

However, Keats might have felt that love could provide an
intense impression of another's identity and be educative in
terms of negative capability by allowing him entrance into a
paradise where disagreeables are evaporated into "the sweetness
of the pain."[8] Yet we know that once he experienced a different feeling; we find its expression in the concluding six lines of
"When I have fears":

> And when I feel, fair creature of an hour,
>   That I shall never look upon thee more,
> Never have relish in the faery power
>   Of unreflecting love!—then on the shore
> Of the wide world I stand alone, and think
> Till Love and Fame to nothingness do sink.

Keats was surely correct when he wrote to Bailey of "a
gordian complication of feelings" about women (*Letters,* I,
342), for here in the ode is a conflict we cannot solve by
examining the relationships shared by the poems, though it is
patent that memories of fair women briefly seen, poetry, philos-

---

[7] In the letter to Reynolds of 11 July 1819, Keats separates what might
be fluttering love and/or imagination and philosophy: In writing of
the new calmness with which he can contemplate worldly failure, he
claims to "have of late been moulting: not for fresh feathers & wings:
they are gone, and in their stead I hope to have a pair of patient sub-
lunary legs." (*Letters,* II, 128).

[8] For a contrary view, see chapter 7, n. 10.

ophy, and love are inextricably tied together in Keats's mind.[9] In this connection it is worth noting again that transportation by intoxication to that paradise represented by the realm of the visionary imagination is rejected as inappropriate when compared to wings of poesy:

> Away! away! for I will fly to thee,
>   Not charioted by Bacchus and his pards,
> But on the viewless wings of Poesy.
>
> ("Ode to a Nightingale," lines 31–33)

The last poem we need to consider is the one "To a Lady Seen for a Few Moments at Vauxhall."

> Time's sea hath been five years at its slow ebb;
>   Long hours have to and fro let creep the sand;
> Since I was tangled in thy beauty's web,
>   And snared by the ungloving of thine hand.
> And yet I never look on midnight sky,
>   But I behold thine eyes' well memoried light;
> I cannot look upon the rose's dye,
>   But to thy cheek my soul doth take its flight;
>   I cannot look on any budding flower,
>   But my fond ear, in fancy at thy lips,
> And harkening for a love-sound, doth devour
>   Its sweets in the wrong sense:—thou dost eclipse
> Every delight with sweet remembering,
> And grief unto my darling joys dost bring.

This sonnet elaborates again the enduring power of beauty momentarily seen to entangle or ensnare. Once again emphasis is placed on brightness, here as in "Fill for me" associated specifically with eyes. Again customary blisses have lost their

---

[9] Compare: "I never was in love—Yet the voice and shape of a woman has haunted me these two days—at such a time when the relief, the feverous relief of Poetry seems much less a crime—This morning Poetry has conquered—I have relapsed into those abstractions which are my only life." (*Letters*, I, 370).

gusto; every delight is made sorrowful by sweetness, and beauty
and joy and melancholy are amalgamated into a single emotional
complex. The paradox in the next-to-the-last line serves to rein-
force this notion: it is *sweet* remembering that brings grief to
joy.

In the group of poems we have been tracing, we have found
that the melancholy aroused by remembering is, paradoxically,
not unpleasant but a consummate experience of intensity. But
there is another group of poems which rejects this consolation.
In this latter group we find that the recollection of past pleasure
quite naturally poisons an already joyless present.

The poem "In a drear-nighted December" provides a fine
example of the more natural or typical experience, but it does so
by denying the familiar romantic relationship between man's
nature and the processes of organic nature.[10]

> In a drear-nighted December,
>   Too happy, happy tree,
> Thy branches ne'er remember
>   Their green felicity:
> The north cannot undo them,
> With a sleety whistle through them;
> Nor frozen thawings glue them
>   From budding at the prime.
>
> In a drear-nighted December,
>   Too happy, happy brook,
> Thy bubblings ne'er remember
>   Apollo's summer look;
> But with a sweet forgetting,
> They stay their crystal fretting,
> Never, never petting
>   About the frozen time.

---

[10] John Middleton Murry's discussion of intensity and the varieties of
indolence is relevant here, though he is not concerned with the sorts
of relationships we are. (p. 204).

> Ah! would 'twere so with many
>   A gentle girl and boy!
> But were there ever any
>   Writh'd not at passed joy?
> The feel of not to feel it,
> When there is none to heal it,
> Nor numbed sense to steal it,
>   Was never said in rhyme.[11]

A very early poem, usually included in the Keats canon but whose authenticity is still a matter of conjecture,[12] "Stay, ruby-breasted Warbler, stay" affirms the relationship between nature and human nature. The use of storms and suggestion of winter help us recognize the poem as Keatsian, even if possibly not Keats's. I shall quote only the last four stanzas, where the addressee is *The emblem of love.*

> When summer nights the dews bestow,
>   And summer suns enrich the day,
> Thy notes the blossoms charm to blow,
>   Each opes delighted at thy lay.

> So when in youth the Eye's dark glance
>   Speaks pleasure from its circle bright,
> The tones of love our joys enhance
>   And make superior each delight.

> And when bleak storms resistless rove,
>   And ev'ry rural bliss destroy,
> Nought comforts then the leafless grove
>   But thy soft note—its only joy—

> E'en so the words of love beguile
>   When Pleasure's tree no flower bears,
> And draw a soft endearing smile
>   Amid the gloom of grief and tears.

---

[11] I follow the text established by Alvin Whitley in the *Harvard Library Bulletin,* V (1951), 116–22.

[12] For discussions of authenticity, see Finney, I, 69–70; Lowell, I, 62–63; and Garrod, 543.

This is, if Keats's, another poem on the pleasures of memory. It explores the antithesis of the drear-nighted December relationships—or, in terms of chronology, the drear-nighted December lyric explores the antithesis of the relationship and significations of "Stay, Ruby-breasted Warbler, stay." In view of Keats's constant explorations of alternatives, we have more internal evidence for the authenticity of the early lyric, but because it does explore a relationship that was a romantic commonplace, we dare not lean too heavily upon it.

The displeasure of memory, which we now see in perspective by antithesis, so straightforwardly expressed in the drear-nighted December lyric is given an added significance in "La Belle Dame sans Merci" where it becomes involved with the realm of the imagination. In order to clarify the relationship in this more complex intellectual environment, let us examine Keats's letter of 15 (?) July 1819. He writes to Fanny Brawne

> I have been reading lately an oriental tale of a very beautiful color—It is of a city of melancholy men, all made so by this circumstance. Through a series of adventures each one of them by turns reach some gardens of Paradise where they meet with a most enchanting Lady ; and just as they are going to embrace her, she bids them shut their eyes—they shut them—and on opening their eyes again find themselves descending to earth in a magic basket. The remembrance of this Lady and their delights lost beyond all recovery render them melancholy for ever after. How I applied this to you, my dear ; how I palpitated at it ; how the certainty that you were in the same world with myself, and though as beautiful, not so talismanic as that Lady ; how I could not bear you should be so you must believe because I swear it by yourself.[13]

It seems plain that Keats draws comfort in the certainty that Fanny's beauty belongs to this world, not another realm, and that memory will not be put to the test of providing an intense joyful melancholy. Now in "La Belle Dame" it may very well

[13] *Letters,* II, 130.

be "the feel of not to feel it" that produces the knight's incurable melancholy. Calm acceptance of this world, in which man must necessarily experience

> his Winter too of pale misfeature
> Or else he would forego his mortal nature,
> ("The Human Seasons," 2nd version, lines 13–14)

is not the way the story ends; the knight is sick unto death in a wintry landscape. The fact that men cannot forget "pass'd joy" is harsh and brutal, though soul-making, and in this group of poems the problem of memory is seen steadily, if not whole. Keats seems to have moved to a realization that only in art, in beautiful Oriental tales, do disagreeables evaporate. Only in the beauty of a sad story is there cathartic relief from the pressure of melancholy feelings.

Appendix

PART A

It is a pleasure to acknowledge the information and inspiration I have gleaned from previous commentators. Often material from their publications has been quoted at length in order that I might avail myself of their perceptions and explanations of the poetry and the mind of John Keats. Nevertheless, I found that occasionally I disagree with parts of their interpretations or conclusions because I have chosen to analyze the poetry primarily in groups of poems which share relationships. Often this position has necessarily emphasized the changes in Keats's attitudes as well as the nuances of successive attitudes. Of course, I am frequently in agreement with conclusions reached by other commentators, and I hope I have not failed to cite any specific agreement. In the cases where application of my method has yielded a standard result, I think two things are accomplished: first, the validity of my method is made plain, and second, additional corroboration is provided for a given reading. As Keats wrote:

But the Minds of Mortals are so different and bent on such diverse Journeys that it may at first appear impossible for any common taste and fellowship to exist . . . between two or three under these suppositions—It is however quite the contrary—Minds would leave each other in contrary directions, traverse each other in Numberless points, and all last greet each other at the Journeys end—A old man and a child would talk together and the old Man be led on his path, and the child left thinking.

Letters, I, 232.

In the first part of this appendix I shall consider generalizations about the mind of Keats insofar as these generalizations concern the putative regularity of his philosophical and attitudinal development or maturation. The second section presents a review of the literature regarding the basic problems of interpreting metaphors, from which I drew the system described in the first chapter. Thirdly I shall consider the techniques of analyzing figurative language and other textural phenomena that have been utilized by other investigators. That this material is placed in the appendix should not be construed as denigrating; I conceive of it rather as supplementary corroboration of the fundamental technique of extracting meaning by analyzing recurring diction in its varying contexts.

The discovery that Keats constantly rethought and refelt his basic problems is not at all startling, but discoveries of this sort have ranged widely over the interpretive possibilities. Some commentators have been primarily concerned with "philosophy" or with Keats's theories of poetry; Hugh I'A. Fausset provides one conclusion about this sort of development. Writing in 1922 he found:

> A close examination of Keats's poetry in the order of its composition, and of his letters in relation to his poetry, revealed to me a very logical and significant development from sensationalism to vision, from idealisation to idealism.
> This gradual definition of his genius, once grasped, should give new point to all he wrote. It makes us more completely one with the intimate dilemmas, the vast potentialities of his abundant nature. His personality, viewed in its struggles for light and for more absolute expression, symbolizes too the everlasting duty of art, and his poetry in all its changing de-

tail ceases to be fortuitous, and reveals an organic unity, to which each particular poem contributes a part, representing a step or stage in the direction of that absolute goal for which we discover Keats to have been aiming.[1]

Four years later, Clarence DeWitt Thorpe challenged the validity of Fausset's discoveries. Thorpe wrote that Fausset "fails in the one object he sets out to accomplish: namely, to show from the poems a progressive development in Keats's poetic principles."[2] Thorpe specifically objects to Fausset's incorrect chronology and his disregard of the letters. I would add that Fausset's failure to consider Keats's so-called minor poetry seriously cripples his method and weakens his conclusions: he is not able to point out the contribution of "each particular poem" as he promises to do. Further, Thorpe asks whether, despite Fausset's self-imposed restriction to a weak chronology and a rather unrepresentative sample of Keats's work, Fausset has not

by his own testimony shown his theory of progressive advancement to be fallacious? Has he not really admitted, what is undubitably true, that in this matter of 'naturalism' and 'idealism' . . . Keats's poetry shows advance and recoil, progress and reaction and interaction, and irregular pendulum-like movement with first one in the ascendancy, then the other?[3]

Thorpe is himself concerned with Keats's theories of poetry. He argues that neither of Keats's two decisive urges—that toward the dream world and that toward a philosophical understanding of the actual world—was ever discarded.[4] Yet he does

---

[1] Fausset, p. 5.

[2] Thorpe, p. 21.

[3] *Ibid.*, p. 23.

[4] *Ibid.*, pp. 91–92. This has been restated by David Perkins, who suggests that "As Keats developed, no major tendency of his imagination was dropped." Perkins, p. 192. This study will help show that the

find that the theory he finally attributes to Keats, and which he considers "eminently satisfactory," is not a theory to which Keats was completely committed. He adds a qualification which, in one sense, is one of the contentions of the present study: "It merely needs to be remarked that he came to his death before he had fully persuaded himself to an emotional acceptance of his reasoned judgment."[5] Only Thorpe's restriction of this conclusion to poetic theory differs in essence from what I have remarked in the introduction about the nature of the reciprocity between philosophy and attitude.

Claude Finney, in the 1936 opus *The Evolution of Keats's Poetry,* indicates even in his title the sense of a final achievement attained in the poetry. But his analyses are not nearly so tendentious as Fausset's, though they are generally far too restrictive philosophically. Finney, however, recognizes the necessity to localize Keats's "holding" of various philosophies of poetry.

> His philosophy of poetry developed, with sudden and frequent reversions and alternations, with amazing rapidity. There is as much change and development in the six years in which he composed poetry as in the sixty-two years of Wordsworth's poetic composition. It is impossible, therefore, to formulate a consistent philosophy of poetry which applies to all of his poems. In no two of his long poems, and in very few of his short poems, did he express the same ideas of life and poetry. In each one of his poems, however, he expressed the ideas which he held on the day or days on which he composed it.[6]

My particular agreements and disagreements with Finney are

---

images which conveyed the tendencies of the imagination were, in fact, as persistent as the ideas themselves, though the expressive functioning of the former changes as the latter alter their intellectual configurations.

[5] *Ibid.,* p. 102.

[6] Finney, I, vii.

noted in the appropriate places in the text, but in general it would be accurate to observe that his interest in sources and philosophy, and his lack of interpretive commentary on the minor poetry, have left me a great deal of territory to explore.

James Caldwell's response to Finney's presentation of Keats's intellectual evolution develops along the lines Thorpe laid out,[7] but he finds even more dynamism in Keats's mind:

> . . . Professor Claude Lee Finney . . . conducts him [Keats] along a sequence of philosophies made to flash across his mind like views of streets from a train window: 'Optimistic naturalism,' given up in the first days of April, 1817, for 'Neo-Platonism,' modified by autumn to 'empirical humanism,' in turn developed by the end of December to 'negative capability,' this rejected by March 13 for 'scepticism,' which slips in the next twelve days to 'pessimism,' displaced on precisely the twenty-fourth of April by 'Wordsworthian humanitarianism,' left behind on October 27 for a return to 'negative capability.'[8]

Caldwell continues:

> This account of a mental career checkered to the point of disrepute is impressively documented, and in a sense, doubtless true. But it is also misleading. It tends to take us away from the realization of a mind infinitely supple, fluent, and diverse, toward a concept of one merely restless in a succession of comfortless attitudes, from a brain teeming, as Keats called his own, toward one jerking from one static arrangement to another with the abrupt and angular movement of a kaleidoscope. The terms and accounts provided in this and similar histories of the poet's mind indicate intellectual structures too stable and ponderous to reflect the animate, nimble configurations which the poems and letters reveal.[9]

---

[7] Caldwell acknowledges this on p. 6.

[8] *Ibid.*, p. 5.

[9] *Ibid.*

Caldwell's conclusions are related primarily to Keats and philosophy, but, if extended, they, like Thorpe's remark, apply equally well to the problems and attitudes I am concerned with in this study:

> Keats indulged at times in other and contradictory speculations. There are in his comments on the imagination traces, indeed, of many trial attitudes, and they indicate perhaps chiefly that he was not primarily concerned with generalizations, with fitting the concept of the imagination into a structure of other concepts.[10]

Amy Lowell's generalization about the proper study of Keats and his works ought to have made Finney's analysis a little less monochromatic, for, as we can see, he utilizes some of her ideas about Keats's constancy. Her statements about Keats's thought and feeling patterns anticipate some of Caldwell's remarks on Keats's conceptualizings.

> Keats was a poet of many moods, of variously tinted shades of thought and feeling. What was true of him at one time was not necessarily true at another, and it is just this tissue of conflicting sensations which we must study and comprehend if we would know the man and his work as both really were, not pigeon-holed into a theoretical pocket, but free and variable as nature itself.[11]

There is yet one more rejoinder to Finney's rigid and over-philosophical ordering of Keats's mind; this recent statement by Bernard Blackstone draws together many of the threads we have seen being unraveled.

> Keats's development is far from being the steady trek from position to position—naturalism, Platonism, humanism, and so on—which some of his critics have made it out to be. It

---

[10] *Ibid.,* pp. 134–35.
[11] Lowell, I, 557.

is much more of a tidal movement, ebbing and flowing; a process of growth, expanding here, contracting there; a systole and diastole, following a natural rhythm. Keats's world is 'the sweet-and-bitter world,' a field for the play of antinomies in thought, feeling, will: a world in which contradictory attitudes can be held in focus together. This is evident in the letters, where he tosses ideas and emotions about like a juggler, squeezing the last drop of entertainment (or wisdom) out of the mood of the moment; it is evident too in the poems, where quite incompatible styles as well as divergent 'philosophies' may mark the work of the same month.[12]

The chapter these remarks introduce discusses Keats's narrative explorations of the theme of sexual strife, but by no means does Blackstone concentrate on the successive adoption of alternative solutions, a process I trace in some detail.

Merely because many of the ideas put forth by Blackstone are not exclusively his does not indicate that they are—or were—shared unanimously by Keatsians. Robert Gittings' 1954 biography, *John Keats: The Living Year,* effectively reasserts the prevalence of the more highly intellectualized sort of philosophical thought in the poetry, though he demonstrates that the philosophy of one moment was not necessarily that of the next; the change is usually attributed to a change in the physical or emotional environment. Discussing the Nightingale and Grecian Urn odes, Gittings remarks:

> It is a larger question whether the philosophy of these poems is also characteristic or whether it was a phase Keats was passing through at the time. This philosophy has a single, coherent, and eternal theme. The poet sees the world as a vale of tears—though Keats, chameleon-fashion, had denied this a fortnight earlier.[13]

Again he writes, "Yet it [the philosophy] is not entirely typical

---

[12] Blackstone, p. 266.
[13] Gittings, *Living Year,* p. 131.

of Keats, nor even of some of his thought just before this time."[14] And of the opposing philosophy of the "vale of Soul-making" Gittings writes:

> This is far more like the robust philosophy which Keats carried out in most practical affairs of his daily life. It must be asked whether there were special circumstances which made him adopt an equally valid but distinctly different philosophy when he wrote the two great odes in the month of May, 1819.[15]

In his later book, *The Mask of Keats,* Gittings seems to extend the range of his recognition of Keats's rapid alternations. He argues that the gusto and intensity of Keats's "participation in all forms of life . . . is somehow lacking . . . in the poems."[16] He continues,

> *The Cap and Bells,* with all its imperfections, is this Keats, the Keats of the Letters, the real chameleon poet, passing in an instant from puns to philosophy and back again—the poet noted by his friend Woodhouse, for whom everything had a life of its own, who could enter into the sensations even of such an object as a billiard-ball.[17]

But it is plain that even here Gittings is not straying too far from the "philosophy" of negative capability. We are removed from attitudes, despite the grounding of the argument in biography.

Douglas Bush's recent biographical study of Keats traces major changes and developments in thought and attitude. Bush, discussing the idea of "man's movement out of the world of illusion into the world of reality," says that "Keats's early craving to 'burst our mortal bars,' to attain through the senses and

---

14 *Ibid.*
15 *Ibid.,* p. 132.
16 *Ibid., Mask of Keats,* p. 142.
17 *Ibid.*

imagination some kind of supramundane or transcendental beauty and truth was, eventually, subdued and chastened by a sober acceptance of the human condition."[18] Bush traces major changes, not the more rapid and subtle alterations I have worked with. His book ends by quoting the conclusions he reached in 1957 (in "Keats and His Ideas," *The Major English Romantic Poets,* ed. C. D. Thorpe et al., Carbondale, Ill., 1957).

For most readers and some critics Keats remains a poet of miraculous sensuous apprehension and magical expression, and in much or most of his poetry, his negative capability seems to stop well short of Shakespearian exploration of life and man, to be mainly confined to aesthetic sensation and intuition. But even if we share that conventional estimate, we must say that his poetry is not all of a piece. Keats's Shakespearian or humanitarian ambitions, his critical and self-critical insights, his acute awareness of the conditions enveloping the modern poet, his struggles toward a vision that would comprehend all experience, joy and suffering, the natural and the ideal, the transient and the eternal—all this made him capable of greater poetry than he actually wrote, and makes him, more than his fellow romantics, our contemporary. And if mere 'ideas' did not get into his poems very often or very far, their overshadowing presence distinguishes his major from his minor achievements. Though his poetry in general was in some measure limited and even weakened by the romantic preoccupation with 'beauty,' his finest writing is not merely beautiful, because he had seen 'the boredom, and the horror' as well as 'the glory.'[19]

As may be gleaned from a close reading of Bush's comments, not much of Keats's poetry conveys ideas very deeply or very successfully. Even the "Ode on Melancholy" and the "Ode to Psyche" "support the old notion of Keats as an epicure of voluptuous sensation. We cannot ask, to be sure, that every

---

[18] Bush, p. 15.
[19] *Ibid.,* p. 212.

short poem should say or imply everything, yet we can hardly fail to recognize in these two odes a relative poverty of theme, however intense the emotions they grow from."[20] Of "Psyche" Bush suggests that "Perhaps Keats's concern here with formal problems made him unaware of how much he had left unsaid or attenuated by a texture and tone of merely or mainly sensuous luxury. He may well have intended to set forth the strong and comprehensive idealism, transcendental or naturalistic, that some critics find, but it is very hard to discern that in the poem he actually wrote."[21]

That it is often difficult to discern Keats's themes is true, but, as I have demonstrated, the difficulty arises from the fact that too often critics overlook the figurative nature of what seems to be merely sensuous luxury. To be sure, by fragmenting figurative relationships Keats made the critics' task harder, but he simultaneously made his poetry not only sensually but also intellectually richer.

Bush, in his attempts to deny philosophic depth to much of Keats's poetry, cites Jack Stillinger's article on "The Eve of St. Agnes" ("The Hoodwinking of Madeline: Scepticism in 'The Eve of St. Agnes,'" *SP*, LVIII [July 1961], 535–55). Bush cites Stillinger as saying that the philosophical interpretation of the poem implies that " 'both Madeline and Porphyro have read *Endymion,* Keats's letters, and the explications of the metaphysical critics.' " This is not fair to Stillinger's article which, through close reading, finds a rather different metaphysical import. Stillinger merely denies that the lovers "are consciously intent on experiencing the conditions of immortality —consciously practicing for the spiritual repetition of pleasure at an even higher level of intensity."[22]

Stillinger concludes his article by examining Keats's faith in the realm of the visionary imagination and his realization that the realities of the world have a valid claim on the poet. Stil-

[20] *Ibid.,* p. 147.
[21] *Ibid.,* p. 132.
[22] Stillinger, p. 537.

linger is not so hostile to the metaphysical critics as Bush would lead us to think: "The metaphysical critics are right in asserting Keats's early trust in the imagination. What they sometimes fail to recognize, themselves eager for glimpses of heaven's bourne, and to an extent hoodwinked with their own rather than Keats's metaphysics, is that before Keats wrote more than a handful of poems we would not willingly let die, he in large part changed his mind."[23]

Nathaniel Teich, in his article "Criticism and Keats's *Grecian Urn,*" argues that

what may happen when mature, reflective critics interpret the poem is that they continue from where Keats left off; they extrapolate the ideas of the poem to conclusions that can only be the critic's own conclusions. In other words, these critics take the philosophically incomplete statements of young Keats and unconsciously complete them by adding their own mature philosophical conclusions.[24]

Stillinger's article also outlines Keats's attitudes toward dreamers and fancy, and it proffers another reason for his contemporaneousness.

The dreamer in Keats is ultimately one who turns his back, not merely on the pains of life, but on life altogether; and in the poems of 1819, beginning with 'The Eve of St. Agnes,' his dreaming is condemned. If the major concern in these poems is the conflict between actuality and the ideal, the result is not a rejection of the actual, but rather a facing up to it that amounts, in the total view, to affirmation. It is a notable part of Keats's wisdom that he never lost touch with reality, that he condemned his hoodwinked dreamers who would shut out the world, that he recognized life as a complexity of pleasure and pain, and laid down a rule for action: achievement of the ripest, fullest experience that one is capable of. These

---

23 *Ibid.,* p. 544.
24 *PQ,* XLIV (Oct. 1965), 502.

qualities make him a saner if in some ways less romantic poet than his contemporaries, and they should qualify him as the Romantic poet most likely to survive in the modern world.[25]

My degree of assent with these ideas can be found in chapter 4. It may be appropriate at this point to reiterate my view that Keats, even latterly, was not so consistent as is implied in Stillinger's conclusion, that I find the poet's contemporaneity in his ambivalences, and that because of Keats's habitual tendency to fragment figurative language so that its very figurativeness is obscured, we ought not disdain metaphysical speculations but encourage wider and deeper reading in order fully to understand the speculative drift of Keats's poems—all his poems.

One side of the discussion of the regularity or irregularity of Keats's philosophical development or of his attitudes has not yet been mentioned; that Keats's feelings maintained a certain fundamental consistency has been presented and is deserving of special mention. Dorothy Van Ghent's 1942 dissertation on "Image Types and Antithetical Structures in the Work of Keats"[26] champions this view. (It does so in a footnote, but to my mind, the wealth of collocation of image traits and their analysis appearing in Mrs. Van Ghent's footnotes are the most fascinating parts of the dissertation.) She writes:

> It is, of course, no part of the purpose of this paper to deal with 'meaning' in the sense of the discrimination of a *rationale* either assumed to have been consciously intended by Keats, or, on the other hand, assumed to be integral to the reader response whether or not intended by Keats. "Hyperion," as an image and emotion complex, is a part of a total context of image and emotion reaching from this poem into and across other poems, a context composed of a limited number of ascertainable affective drives and a limited number of ascertainable image-types; the critical weighing of a *rationale*

---

[25] Stillinger, p. 555.
[26] Unpublished. (University of California, Berkeley)

assumed to be proper to "Hyperion" itself would appear to be irrelevant to this total context. Keats felt no consistency in his own *opinions* . . . but the consistency of his feelings has quantitative proof, by virtue of repetition through poem after poem.[27]

Now the first thing that needs to be noted is that the image-traits Mrs. Van Ghent considers are put into two broad categories, which they undeniably fit: repose forms and unrest forms. There can be no quarrel with her conclusions regarding the psychological structure of Keats's mind as holding these broadly warring contraries in a unified tension, for others, though more impressionistically, have made the same observations. It should also be noted that merely because her technique "deals only in the second or third place with apparent philosophies (such philosophies as are generally equated with 'meaning' in a poem)"[28] this does not preclude the analysis of meaning by examination of the local contexts of images.

We can continue the examination of attitudes rather than philosophies by picking up one of the more recent threads in Keats criticism: the dramatic. Two kinds of dramaticism are involved: one is found within the succession of attitudes expressed in a single poem—which is the focus of most current explications—and the other is roughly domiciled in what seems to be the distance between the poet and the poem. Of the latter, E. C. Pettet writes:

. . . when we read some of the most personal of Keats's lyrics . . . we feel that while these poems are thoroughly Romantic, they are only momentarily, and not typically, Keatsian. And sometimes, as notably in the 'Bright Star' sonnet, there is a curious blend of objective writing and a romantic confessional outpouring in the same lyric.[29]

[27] Van Ghent, p. 135, n. 2.

[28] *Ibid.*, p. 227.

[29] Pettet, p. 287.

Pettet also comments on the first variety of dramaticism, and in doing so he posits a healthy attitude to adopt toward the bulk of Keats's poetry.

> Though often naïve, it is not simple or shallow, for as we have indicated in several of the previous chapters it is ravelled with complex impulses and ambivalences, like the love of death and the 'gordian complication of feelings' about women, that fascinate and take us deep into the secret places of the human heart.[30]

Even more assertive, though at the same time even more mystical, is Bernice Slote's statement:

> The poems of Keats—the life and the writing—are both mingled and separate. And it is pertinent to both the study of Keats and the study of poetry to observe how their natures are defined and how they are informed by the dramatic principle: that is, act by imaginative identities, the objective playing-out of the clash of oppositions.[31]

In picking up this thread of criticism we are not neglecting "philosophies." It was Earl Wasserman who applied the dramatistically oriented view to Keats's underlying philosophical conceptions, or, better still, who perceived that "At most, his poetry is descriptive and suppositive, not prescriptive. He will examine the consequences of an hypothesis . . . but he will not have a palpable design on us by causing his poetry to prescribe one mode of existence rather than another."[32] If hypothesis can mean not only philosophical but emotional assumptions, it is plain that I agree with Wasserman.

Mary Visick's article " 'Tease us out of Thought': Keats's *Epistle to Reynolds* and the Odes," compares the Nightingale, Grecian Urn, and Autumn odes, as well as other major poems,

---

[30] *Ibid.*, p. 355.
[31] Slote, p. 9.
[32] Wasserman, p. 163.

and the epistle in terms of Keats's attempts to reconcile imagination and philosophy. She does not attempt to explicate the epistle; rather she is concerned with some of Keats's "half-formed images" which "although he has not completely apprehended them he seems at least to use [them] . . . as a means of exploring certain territory . . . he has already mapped." She finds that the images "express both his need of romance and his growing conviction . . . that it is inadequate. Until, in the odes, he completely realizes these images, he worries them, as he does most notably in this verse letter. The strife between Romance and 'the love of good and ill' teases him out of thought."[33] Miss Visick's article is concerned more with pictorial images as symbols than with the sort of investigation I am pursuing, and her ideas of Keats's philosophizing seem tissue thin, especially when compared with those of Wasserman.

However, the survey itself cannot end with this; we must come nearly full circle, back to the idea of a "steady evolving whole." It is Pettet who finds in the Keats canon that

> . . . poem grows out of poem in a quite remarkable way, and the more important ones are usually rich in cross-references. Considered together, the poems leave an impression, as perhaps only Wordsworth's work among the other Romantic Poets does, of one steadily evolving whole. We can perhaps appreciate this quality of Keats's poetry best by placing it beside Shelley's, which, great as it is, reveals a chaotic, zigzag, and often random development.[34]

It is one of the contentions of this monograph that Keats's development, though development there may have been, was as arbitrary in some areas as Pettet claims Shelley's to have been. Further, I have shown a great deal more cross-reference between minor poems than exists in "the more important ones." And I hope I have not spoken of steadily evolving wholes without defining them.

---

33 *K-SJ*, XV (1966), pp. 87–98.
34 Pettet, p. 42.

One such whole has been defined and traced by Walter Evert, though it is one evolved not only toward but from. There are several reasons for treating it last. First, it too returns to the idea that Keats did have a tenable, relatively stable, and permanent philosophy. Second, it is found in one of the most recent books on Keats. Third, the method by which Evert traced the philosophy is very similar to the method I use in tracing other relationships. (I am, of course, highly pleased that he concentrated on the single though manifold relationship involving such components as: Apollo, West, sunset, evening, gold, harmony, harvest, and natural sounds.)

One of Evert's primary arguments is "that Keats did systematize his perceptions and that he was governed, through much of his poetic career, by the system he had formulated."[35] The main difference between the system Evert has discovered and those discovered by previous scholars is that this system is "rooted in analogy, and, while it pretended to a certain consecutiveness at its upper levels, its logic was built upon analogies among data not properly comparable."[36] The system itself is not my concern,[37] but the method Evert uses surely is. Discussing Keats's "central formulation," he writes:

> As the poet never gave it complete expression in any one place, it has been inferred from partial explanations and repeated allusions throughout the early poetry and from occasional hints in the letters. That Keats held such a view one infers from its touchstone quality, for virtually everything he wrote, through *Endymion,* conforms to its pattern, and some passages that have baffled commentators are reduced by its means to perfect comprehensibility—without, of course, becoming better poetry by that means.[38]

In much the same way I think that the tracing and explicat-

---

[35] Evert, p. 7.
[36] *Ibid.*
[37] For a summary of the system, see *Ibid.*, pp. 30–32.
[38] *Ibid.*, p. 30.

ing of other fragmented relational systems elucidates much poetry which, if not baffling, has been largely and unwisely ignored.

Evert's book also provides another definition of the whole toward which Keats's poetry steadily evolved. He writes that

> almost all writers on Keats have commented on the extent of verbal recurrence in his works, formal and informal, and the present study has been much concerned with one of the most pervasive of these patterns. One might hope too for agreement that Keats's work does in many ways constitute an organic whole, that he frequently returns to former themes and reworks them, in effect holding dialogues with himself in which he matches his current level of understanding against an earlier view of the same subject.[39]

I am inclined to agree with this sort of definition of an organic whole, though I think the implication false that current levels of understanding are both more permanent and more mature than earlier levels. The present study will, I hope, further the sort of agreement Evert hopes for, with only the reservations noted above.

Keats's figurative language has been the focus of many studies, most of which are directed toward elucidating a specific problem; for example, see Mario D'Avanzo's recent dissertation on "Recurrent Metaphors for Poetry in John Keats's Work."[40] While of considerable importance, this sort of investigation, and studies of recurrent diction and imagery like those of Perkins and Pettet,[41] and Dorothy Van Ghent's study

---

[39] *Ibid.*, p. 250.

[40] Unpublished. (Brown University, 1963) I regret that the book D'Avanzo made of his dissertation appeared after my work on this book was nearly completed, for there is much we share in our approach to Keats's poetry. Nevertheless, our emphases are quite different.

[41] See Perkins' article in *K-SJ*, II (1953), 51–60; and Pettet, chapter 2.

discussed in the first section, are not directed toward the same end or focused on the same kinds of figurative language as is this study.

Although there are no studies that focus exclusively on the thematic significance of fragmented relationships, a growing sense of such significance can be traced. M. R. Ridley's 1933 *Keats' Craftmanship* concerns itself largely with the effectiveness of Keats's imagery in arousing reader response to sensory stimuli: he is interested in Keats's power to make us feel, touch, taste, hear, and see. Two extracts from his book are sufficient to indicate its methods, aims, and conclusions.

> As we have studied *The Eve of St. Agnes* in considerable detail, and shall be watching again Keats' methods of verbal 'carpentry' in the *Ode to a Nightingale* and in *To Autumn,* and as such study easily becomes wearisome, I propose for examination in this Ode [Psyche] no more than some examples of that process of 'distillation' by which Keats manages to concentrate in one line or phrase the full rich essence of images which have hitherto found only partial expression in scattered passages in his earlier work.[42]

Ridley concludes his examination of the *Ode to Psyche* with the following passage, in which I have italicized the words indicating his emphasis on the sensory expressiveness of rich, essential images.

> No wonder that with this power of 'distillation' at work the poem has about it a *richness* new in Keats' work, and wholly different from that *lusciousness,* the product of an unchecked exuberance, which marked, and often marred, his earlier work. He has learned to make the true attar, and though he may not always succeed in making it, he is never again going to be content with anything more *dilute.*[43]

Some of James Caldwell's general conclusions about the na-

---

[42] Ridley, p. 193.
[43] *Ibid.,* p. 195.

ture of Keats's mind were presented in the first section of this appendix, but his comments on the precise workings of Keats's mind are of great importance in demonstrating the exact way in which image and idea are the reality of one another, are interchangeable in the poet's mind and in his poetry. Caldwell's analysis and description of the processes at work provide the psychological explanation for the existence of fragmented relationships, that is, relationships all of whose terms do not achieve meaningful expression in a particular poem. Of an associative chain of ideas in Keats's letter of 17 December 1818 to Charles Cowden Clarke, he notes:

> What is most interesting is that here he gives a more or less local habitation and name ('The common place Book of my Mind') to that fluent, lawless, vivid welter of stored ideas whence all these valuable intrusions are drawn. This is, of course, the associative process, the imagination, or as we now call it, the stream of consciousness. William James' description of it is classic, and worth recalling; for it stresses the fact which Keats realized, with extraordinary psychological insight, of the constant activity and interplay of this stream in all kinds of thinking. Every definite image in the mind is steeped and dyed in the free water that flows around it. With it goes the sense of its relations, near and remote, the dying echo[44] whence it came to us, the dawning sense of whither it is to lead. The significance, the value of the image is in this halo or penumbra that surrounds and escorts it.[45]

Caldwell concludes by establishing that the "simple imaginative mind" freely substitutes image for idea:

> Its mighty abstract ideas are modes of operation—frankly conveyed—in the 'halo or penumbra that surrounds and escorts' the subject. They evolve as the poems evolve from the free work of the associative principle. The striking thing is

---

[44] In chapter 4 above we had occasion to recall this image in connection with some of Keats's poetry.

[45] Caldwell, pp. 146–47.

that Keats dares allow them to stand alone, and without the supporting convention of poetry, that he dares 'think' as well as dream with his imagination.[46]

A modern critic comes to a strikingly similar conclusion about the way in which Keats thought. Cleanth Brooks finds in the odes "an integration of intellect and emotion. Form *is* meaning. The thinking goes on through the images and receives its precise definition and qualification through the images."[47] Unlike Caldwell, Brooks has "no theory to offer concerning Keats's psychology of composition,"[48] yet he too finds

> that the imagery, however spontaneously it may have come to Keats's mind, was shaped, consciously or unconsciously, by that mind to a precision that is beautifully exact. The poems seem to me inexhaustibly rich. Even if the sensuous detail was the conscious preoccupation of the poet, the detail as given is more than that: it teases us *into* thought. . . .[49]

What seems to me even more striking than thinking in images is that even within the conventions of poetry Keats often allows only part of an imaginal or relational cluster to stand alone representing an idea or theme.[50] Probably because the ideas and the images in which they are conveyed were so familiar to Keats he did not sense that his audience did not share the same comfortable familiarity. The familiarity the poet might have felt probably stems from the fact that most of the stream is underground: the associations are not primarily conscious.

---

[46] *Ibid.*, p. 157.

[47] Cleanth Brooks, "The Artistry of Keats," in *The Major English Romantic Poets: A Symposium in Reappraisal,* ed. Thorpe, Baker, and Weaver (Carbondale, Ill., 1957), p. 251. His italics.

[48] *Ibid.*

[49] *Ibid.* His italics.

[50] Compare the extract from Murry quoted in the second part of the appendix.

Edward Armstrong's discussion of Shakespeare's imagination uses a line from a Keats letter to document a major conclusion, and his discussion illuminates further the area of thematic significance; in some respects the following extracts amplify Caldwell's insights. Armstrong argues that analysis of thematic imagery

> illustrates several of the most characteristic features of Shakespeare's memory. (1) An apparently insignificant cue may initiate the recall of a very extensive series of images. As Keats said in connection with the association of ideas— 'merely pulling an apron string we set a pretty peal of chimes at work.' (2) Once a theme or interest assumes importance it tends to recur and become integrated into the texture of the play. (3) The associations of the images are not achieved mainly on the conscious level.[51]

In these things too, it may not be too daring to fancy Shakespeare to be Keats's Presider.[52]

Armstrong's conclusions about the persistence and modifications of imaginal relationships are important in demonstrating that the method of investigation I have pursued and my conclusions are not eccentric since in Shakespeare too similar thematic concerns are expressed early and late in similar images.

> It is of the essential nature of an imaginal cluster to be held together over a considerable space of time, though the organisation of its components may be subject to modification, and therefore it is apparent that it undergoes the process which we call 'incubation.' It is the product of remembered emotional and intellectual elements. The rational element is patent from the fashion in which linkages established in earlier plays are integrated into later work by Shakespeare, and we have already noted that emotion is active in creating and maintain-

---

[51] Armstrong, p. 115.
[52] See the letter of 11 May 1817 to Haydon for this phrase as Keats uses it.

ing some, and possibly most, clusters. Thus these linkages represent in miniature the functions involved in all imagination—memory, emotion, and reason.[53]

Despite his emphasis on proving that Wieland's *Oberon* was perhaps the most influential of Keats's sources, Werner Beyer's book helps to establish even more firmly that similar textural details often overlay structural similarities. He argues that

> *Oberon* reveals the close interdependence of many poems he [Keats] wrote, in virtue of their visibly over-lapping patterns. Repeatedly the poems show how in the same passages he sought material or stimulation; how his mind often reverted to the same scenes—with similar or else totally different results. The same inspiration affected him differently at nearly the same time or at widely separated periods. But the diverse as well as the kindred results point out unsuspected relationships among poems which on the surface seem utterly unrelated in topic or time.[54]

Some textural details may not, at first glance, seem sufficiently relevant to a discussion of their thematic or expressive significance. But, as Dorothy Van Ghent points out,

> in describing palaces, it is not a circumstantial necessity to describe portals as well, nor in describing portals is it a circumstantial necessity to open them. We have witnessed before the importance, by force of recurrent phraseology and a recurrent minor ornament, of the whole design, both in large and in detail, of these habitual notations.[55]

Perhaps the materials of my investigation may be summed up by Earl Wasserman's description of the "Ode on a Grecian

---

[53] Armstrong, p. 147.
[54] Beyer, p. 288.
[55] Van Ghent, p. 146.

Urn" and "La Belle Dame": "both are *variant artistic inter-textures* of the three co-existent themes that dominate Keats' deepest meditations and profoundest system of values."[56]

Yet to be examined are the contributions of specific critics to the theoretical basis of this study. This section discusses problems involved in describing and analyzing figurative language, and is not directly related, through the use of examples, to the poetry of Keats.

Stephen J. Brown's book, *The World of Imagery: Metaphor and Kindred Imagery* (London, 1927), posits for us the essential concept of relations.

> The truth, therefore, of a given metaphor depends upon the truth of an implied equation, an equation not between two objects belonging to different spheres of being (life and a river, for instance, or moral degradation and mire), but between two relations, or, to use a mathematical term, two *ratios*. The mind perceives an analogy between these two relations and uses one as an illustration of the other. But may we not carry our analysis a stage further and inquire into the nature of this perceived analogy that is at the back of metaphor? [57]

Father Brown continues:

> Strictly speaking, then, metaphor consists not merely, as does all analogy, in a proportion (an equation of simple ratios), but in a proportion between the proportions.[58]

As an example he offers the following: Apostles are the light of the world.

---

[56] Wasserman, p. 83. Italics added.
[57] Brown, p. 70.
[58] *Ibid.*

$$\frac{A}{X} \qquad \frac{B}{Y}$$

$$\frac{C}{C^1} \qquad \frac{E}{E^1}$$

In the first proportion, A represents the Apostles as preachers of Christianity; who are to B, the enlightenment of men's minds and hearts, as C cause is to E effect. In the second proportion, light, X, is to Y, the lighting up of surrounding objects as C^1 Cause, is to E^1 effect. Father Brown concludes:

> That is to say, light and the Apostles as preachers of the Christian religion are related to one another, analogous to one another as causes; just as physical and moral enlightenment are related to one another, analogous to one another, as effects.[59]

I. A. Richards in analyzing "the philosophy of rhetoric" in his book of the same name is similarly concerned with relations. But before he discusses this aspect of metaphor, he establishes clearly that figurative language involves more than the communication of sensory data, though it may have its roots in such an attempt, and that more than the traditional notion of embellishment is normally required of metaphor.

> A modern theory would object, first, that in many of the most important uses of metaphor, the co-presence of the vehicle and tenor[60] results in a meaning (to be clearly distinguished from the tenor) which is not obtainable without their interaction. That the vehicle is not normally a mere embellishment of a tenor which is otherwise unchanged by it

---

[59] *Ibid.*, pp. 72–73.

[60] Richards has identified the tenor as "the underlying idea or principal subject which the vehicle or figure means." *The Philosophy of Rhetoric* (New York, 1936), p. 97.

but that vehicle and tenor in cooperation give a meaning of more varied powers than can be ascribed to either. And a modern theory would go on to point out that with different metaphors the relative importance of the contributions of vehicle and tenor to this resultant meaning varies immensely. At one extreme the vehicle may become almost a mere decoration or coloring of the tenor, at the other extreme the tenor may become almost a mere excuse for the introduction of the vehicle, and so no longer be 'the principal subject.' And the degree to which the tenor is imagined 'to be that very thing which it only resembles' also varies immensely.[61]

Richards has now prepared the ground for the most vital part of his discussion, that involving the various kinds of relations and the interpretive strategies by which we may begin to analyze them.

Once we begin 'to examine attentively' interactions which do not work through *resemblances* between tenor and vehicle, but depend upon other relations between them including *disparities,* some of our most prevalent, over-simple, ruling assumptions about metaphors as comparisons are soon exposed.[62]

This discussion is amplified by the following remarks:

Let us consider, now, some of the varying relations between tenor and vehicle. It is convenient to begin with the remark, which you will meet with everywhere, that a metaphor includes a comparison. What is a comparison? It may be several different things: it may be just a putting together of two things to let them work together; it may be a study of them both to see how they are like and how unlike one another; or it may be a process of drawing attention to certain aspects of the one through the co-presence of the other.[63]

---

61 *Ibid.,* pp. 100–101.
62 *Ibid.,* pp. 107–8. His italics.
63 *Ibid.,* p. 120.

W. K. Wimsatt's approval of W. B. Stanford's definition of metaphor prompts him to comment on the importance of the context of metaphors.

> The theorist of poetry tends more and more today to make metaphor the irreducible element of his definition of poetry, but in attempting to define metaphor itself he tends further-more to shoot off into an endlessly interesting series of meta-phors. Let me draw to a conclusion by calling attention to one of the most precise attempts to define metaphor which I know, that of W. B. Stanford in his *Greek Metaphor: Studies in Theory and Practice* (Oxford, 1936). Metaphor, he says, is

>> the process and result of using a term (X) normally sig-nifying an object or concept (A) in such a context that it must refer to another object or concept (B) which is distinct enough in characteristics from A to ensure that in the composite idea formed by the synthesis of the concepts A and B and now symbolized in the word X, the factors A and B retain their conceptual independence even while they merge in the unity symbolized by X.[64]

> And this process, result, or situation is one upon which Stanford confers the happily conceived metaphoric name *stereoscope of ideas.* A poem itself, I shall venture to add, is the *context* of Stanford's description. It is a structure of verbal meaning which keeps a metaphor alive, that is, which holds the focal terms A and B in such a way that they remain distinct and illuminate each other, instead of collapsing into literalness. (That this structure itself will participate in the color of the metaphor may be asserted, but need not here be specifically elaborated.)[65]

It does need here to be specifically elaborated because we are concerned with the different meanings of a figurative relation-ship as these are colored by context, and, moreover, with the reciprocal nature of this latter transaction. Discussing "Freud

---

[64] (Kentucky, 1954), p. 127, quoting Stanford.
[65] Wimsatt, p. 128. His italics.

and the Analysis of Poetry," Kenneth Burke suggests a critical methodology by which we can investigate textural phenomena.

> The critic should adopt a variant of the free-association method. One obviously cannot invite an author, especially a dead author, to oblige him by telling what the author thinks of when the critic isolates some detail or other for improvisation. But what he can note is the context of imagery and ideas in which an image takes its place. He can also note, by such analysis, the kinds of evaluations surrounding the imagery of a crossing; for instance, is it an escape from or a return to an evil or a good, etc.? Until finally, by noting the ways in which this crossing behaves, what subsidiary imagery accompanies it, what kind of event it grows out of, what kind of event grows out of it, what altered rhythmic and tonal effects characterize it, etc., one grasps its significance as motivation. And there is no essential motive offered here. The motive of the work is equated with the structure of interrelationships within the work itself.[66]

Later in the same chapter, Burke describes the occurrence of what I would call fragmented relationships, and his description once again establishes the more general validity of the method I have developed for their analysis.

> It is obvious that such structural interrelationships can not be wholly conscious, since they are generalizations about acts that can only be made inductively and statistically after the acts have been accumulated. (This applies as much to the acts of a single poem as to the acts of many poems. We may find a theme emerging in one work that attains fruition in that same work—the ambiguities of its implications where it first emerges attaining explication in the same integer. Or its full character may not be developed until a later work. In its ambiguous emergent form it is a synecdochic representative of the form it later assumes when it comes to fruition in either the same work or another one.)[67]

[66] Burke, *The Philosophy of Literary Form* (Baton Rouge, 1941), p. 267.
[67] *Ibid.,* pp. 279–80.

PART B

It seems to me appropriate to include the results of investigations by other Keatsians, results which are the products of a similar method. This will serve not only to demonstrate again the validity of the technique I have applied, but also, and I think more importantly, these extracts bring into my study comments about poems and relationships I omitted because they had been discussed by previous commentators. Perhaps the value of this study to others will thus be enhanced.

It is interesting to note that most of the commentary is about major poems; often the same sets of relationships have been traced by more than one critic. Also interesting is the general agreement that (1) Keats reused imaginal material in a manner increasingly significant in sensory and intellectual experiences, and (2) that we are frequently presented with alternative actions, reversals of strategy, or palinodes. Some of the chains of evidence are simply too lengthy or too diffuse to quote, while some seem to be nearly intuitive leaps to a truth. In the case of the former, I have cited only the conclusions and the general location of the evidence in the hope that the interested reader will be stimulated to reread the passages in the original.

Beginning with one of the seemingly intuitive leaps we may note Newell F. Ford's recognition of thematic reversal in "La Belle Dame" and "The Eve of St. Agnes."

> The song which awoke Madeline was 'La belle dame sans mercy.' Everyone knows Keats's later poem on the same subject, where a lover's 'fond imagination' betrays and cheats him, even as Endymion in despairing moments believed that his imagination was deceiving him. The poem called 'La Belle Dame' is thus the very palinode to the idea that the imagination is veraciously prefigurative. But in 'The Eve of St. Agnes' the ditty known as 'La belle dame sans mercy' . . . awakens her to the 'truth' of her dream.[1]

---
[1] Ford, p. 128.

Far more detailed and far more philosophically oriented are the interpretations of Keats's major poems by Earl Wasserman, but it must be recalled that he recognizes—specifically in the case of the "Ode on a Grecian Urn" and "La Belle Dame"— that they "both are variant artistic intertextures of the three coexistent themes that dominate Keats' deepest meditations and profoundest system of values."[2] The three are the concept of the pleasure thermometer, the mystic oxymoron of heaven's bourne, and annihilation of self. Wasserman points out interpoem and intra-poem reversals in his analysis of "The Eve of St. Agnes."

> In the two poems we have already examined ["La Belle Dame" and the "Ode on a Grecian Urn"], Keats allowed the intrusion of the mutable world to dispel his vision of heaven. But in 'The Eve of St. Agnes' he is concerned with pressing forward into the consequences of coalescing mortal experience and the condition of immortality, not with tracing the homeward journey of mortality to its habitual self, as he did in 'La Belle Dame Sans Merci' and the 'Ode on a Grecian Urn.' Therefore the perception of the mortal Porphyro only *'nigh* expell'd / The blisses' of Madeline's dream. Having threatened to recall Madeline to mortality, Keats now reverses his strategy. Granted that in this world beauty is not truth, let us assume, he proposes, that mortality could rise to such heights that the difference between the two Porphyro's [sic] would be blotted out because the intensity of his mortal passions would then correspond to the intensity of his spiritual repetition. Madeline would be no longer torn between truth and beauty, for the two would coincide; and the ideal Madeline and the human Porphyro could unite to experience the conditions of heaven.[3]

Wasserman's comments on the thematic materials of the nightingale ode and the "Ode on a Grecian Urn" have a similar cast.

---

2 Wasserman, p. 83.

3 *Ibid.,* pp. 108–9.

Briefly, we are to read it [the nightingale ode] by an inversion of the perspectives that give the 'Ode on a Grecian Urn' its meaning. Or, better, we are to recognize the irony whereby Keats translates the experience with the nightingale into the terms of one who is being drawn back to the mortal world, and not one who, as in the other ode, is progressing towards the bourne of heaven. The thematic materials of the two odes . . . are the same; but what blends organically in the 'Ode on a Grecian Urn' disintegrates in this ode; what is seen in its immortal aspects in the former is seen in its mortal aspects in the latter.[4]

John Middleton Murry's long account of the genesis and growth of the image and idea complex in the Chapman's *Homer* sonnet is, perhaps, too well known to require extensive quotation, but the conclusions he reaches are, as I pointed out in the first part of the appendix, similar to those of James Caldwell, and, as such, deserve repetition here. Having traced Keats's association of Nature and poetry, his use of the ardor of exploration and the excitement of discovery, and his response to the ocean and the moon prior to the composition of the sonnet, Murry concludes:

His two crowning sense-discoveries were those of the moon and sea, and those are instantly pressed into the service of his thought: the images of the moon and the ocean can serve at will to embody the objects of his thought. And he is able to think more exactly concerning the nature of poetry because the sensuous images of moon and ocean are become true symbols of the reality about which he is thinking. So that in the process of unconscious elaboration the continually progressing thought is ever given fresh definition and substance by the images it is able to assimilate; and, on the other hand, the images acquire a thought-content. The thought steadily gains focus and intensity; the images significance.[5]

---

[4] *Ibid.*, p. 184.
[5] Murry, p. 164.

Another biographically oriented Keatsian is Robert Gittings, whose identifications have both illuminated some dark poems and shocked their virtuous commentators. One of the least controversial is the identification of Bellanaine in "The Cap and Bells" with Fanny Brawne, for which, Gittings says,

> there is some good evidence. Mr. Middleton Murry says, somewhat surprisingly, that Bellanaine is an anagram of Annabella—a statement that will at once be refuted by any crossword enthusiast. The name is a clear combination of Italian and French—bella naine—beautiful Dwarf, the exact counterpart of Keats himself, who styled himself as 'the dwarf', and who had noted about Fanny when he first met her 'She is about my height.' Keats this autumn was in the throes, not only of thwarted sexual desire about Fanny, but of jealousy: it is to be remembered that the sub-title of the poem, which he preferred, was to be *The Jealousies*. The stanza which deals with Bellanaine's infidelities is particularly striking, when we compare it with what Keats himself wrote to Fanny.

> There he says plainly that she loved a man!
> That she around him flutter'd, flirted, toy'd,
> Before her marriage with great Elfinan;
> That after marriage too, she never joy'd
> In husband's company, but still employ'd
> Her wits to 'scape away to Angle-land;
> Where liv'd the youth, who worried and annoy'd
> Her tender heart, and its warm ardour's fann'd
> To such a dreadful blaze, her side would scorch her hand.

Keats in his *Ode to Fanny,* written at almost this exact time, has two stanzas:

> Why, this—you'll say, my Fanny! is not true:
>   Put your soft hand upon your snowy side,
> Where the heart beats: confess—'tis nothing new—
>   Must not a woman be
>   A feather on the sea

> Sway'd to and fro by every wind and tide?
>   As blow-ball from the mead?
>
> I know it—and to know it is despair
>   To one who loves you as I love, sweet Fanny!
> Whose heart goes fluttering for you every where,
>   Nor when away you roam,
>   Dare keep its wretched home,
> Love, Love, alone has pains severe and many:
>   Then, loveliest! keep me free,
>   From torturing jealousy.

The images and feeling of these two pieces of description are almost identical.[6]

Not all of E. C. Pettet's methods or conclusions are acceptable to me, as I have tried to indicate previously. It remains for me to cite two instances of his investigation of imagery that are not subject to my earlier criticisms that he remains too interested in proving Keats's utter fascination and skill with sensuous poetry. The first instance of thematic concern occurs in Pettet's discussion of imaginal correspondences between stanzas II and IV of the "Ode to a Nightingale" and the Indian Maid's song of sorrow in "Endymion" book IV. He concludes:

> In the light of these correspondences there can be little doubt that the transitions between stanzas II and IV in the ode approximately follow these of the imaginary Indian Maid in a poem of two years earlier and that Keats was to some extent repeating in these two stanzas an old complex of ideas, sentiments, and images. Further, the recapitulation points to a criticism of this part of the ode: it looks as though Keats in his desperate attempt to flee from the 'weariness, the fever, and the fret' is regressing into an earlier, immature attitude that he had mainly abandoned.[7]

---

[6] *Mask of Keats*, pp. 139–40. Stanza XII of "The Cap and Bells" is quoted.
[7] Pettet, p. 265.

I am not convinced that this is a fair criticism of the ode. While we may not feel that escape to heaven's bourne is mature, we may not be entitled to judge poetry by such standards, at least not completely. Besides, it seems to me that in this ode particularly Keats comes to a realization that the bourne of heaven if attainable can not remain so for long unless we sacrifice our mortality, a sacrifice which, as I have suggested earlier, is not possible because if in death one becomes a sod, then this is not the beautiful, luxurious death envisioned by the immature Keats. It is interesting to note that the two scholars who plump for the sensuous Keats as opposed to the philosophic finally cannot agree which poetry they prefer: Pettet does not like Keats's flights away from earth; Garrod thinks Keats fails when describing reality.

Considerable attention has been paid to the imagery of sacrifice in the "Ode on a Grecian Urn" and parallel imagery in other poems. Comparing "Endymion" book I and the ode, Pettet argues that the

> image of sacrificial rites on a 'pious morn' is certainly not digressive or merely decorative. Deriving from his belief in a Golden Age at the time of the ancient Greeks, it stands for communal happiness, and is thus complementary with his picture of ideal and individual felicity in the two previous stanzas.[8]

Dorothy Van Ghent in one of her interesting footnotes comments more extensively on the antecedents of stanza IV.

> In an "Epistle to John Hamilton Reynolds," the priest, the lowing heifer, and also the pipes of the first and second stanzas of the "Urn" appear as images in the stream of association, along with 'Alexander with his nightcap on' and Hazlitt playing with Miss Edgeworth's cat':

---

[8] *Ibid.,* p. 339.

> The sacrifice goes on; the pontiff knife
> Gleams in the sun, the milk-white heifer lows,
> The pipes go shrilly, the libation flows . . .
>
> (lines 20–2)

In 'Endymion,' the garlanded procession, the altar, the priest, and the ditties and the 'fair creatures' of the earlier stanzas of the 'Urn', as well as the marble in which they are preserved, appear in the context of the religious celebration and the hymn to Pan in Book I. I shall merely quote the pertinent references:

> A troop of little children garlanded;
> Who gathering round the altar . . .
>
> (lines 110–11)
>
> A venerable priest full soberly,
> Begirt with ministring looks . . .
>
> (lines 149–50)
>
> . . . shepherds, lifting in due time aloud
> Their share of the ditty. After them appear'd
> Up-followed by a multitude. . . .
>
> (lines 162–64)

(Here Endymion makes his appearance and the hymn to Pan is chanted.)

> Meantime, on shady levels, mossy fine,
> Young companies nimbly began dancing
> To the swift treble pipe, and humming string.
> Aye, those fair living forms swam heavenly
> To tunes forgotten—out of memory:
> Fair creatures! . . .
> . . . . not yet dead
> But in old marbles ever beautiful.
>
> (lines 312–19)

Here, scattered through some two hundred lines, are most of the pictorial elements of the 'Grecian Urn,' together with some of the diction. Between the little children and the priest are some young damsels

> Such as sat listening round Apollo's pipe
> When the great deity, for earth too ripe,
> Let his divinity o'er-flowing die
> In music, through the vales of Thessaly . . .
> (lines 141–44)

the citation I have already made from 'Endymion' in connection with the 'Ode to a Nightingale' and the out-pouring of the soul as music is out-poured. There is here, then, somewhat of a patchwork of elements later woven into both the 'Urn' and the 'Nightingale.' The separation of these elements in the two later poems is, of course, the result of the selection exercised by mood and subject; but their mixture here indicates their affinity. This, observed in specific materials, is some slight evidence of the general underlay of affinity I have been tracing among the odes. More significantly, it is an indication of the early formation of certain complex configurations of imagery and attended emotion, that is, certain specific imaginal habits, preserved intact in contour over a number of years and operative fairly at random within one context of subject-matter and now within another.[9]

Mrs. Van Ghent is able to draw many interesting and significant conclusions from parallel image-traits. For example, in a note following her explication of the Nightingale ode she writes:

> That the pattern, or at least some of the significant parts of the pattern I have traced here in the "Ode to a Nightingale," is not contingent upon a set of natural observations and a related set of emotions which impinged upon the sensibility of Keats on a day in May in 1819, at Wentworth Place, when he heard a nightingale singing nearby, may be illustrated by citation from other poems where pieces of the same pattern, both sensible and ideational, are manifested.
>   Most near in diction, as well as—taken together—clearly defining the chief outlines of the 'Ode', are the following: In 'Endymion,' there are the lines

---

[9] Van Ghent, pp. 49–50. Compare this with Werner Beyer's statement.

> . . . birds from coverts innermost and drear
> warbling for very joy mellifluous sorrow—
>
> > > (III, 470–71)

where an opposition of emotions associated with the song of
birds, and where the birds themselves, like the nightingale of
the 'Ode,' are in 'coverts innermost.' In 'The Eve of St.
Agnes,' the eloquence of the nightingale is associated with
death, and with death in a 'dell':

> . . . . . her heart was voluble,
> Paining with eloquence her balmy side;
> As though a tongueless nightingale should swell
> Her throat in vain; and die, heart-stifled,
>
> > > in her dell.
> > > > (Stanza XXIII)

In 'Endymion' again, the same phenomenon occurs, in image,
as in stanza VI of the 'Ode' ('Now more than ever seems it
rich to die . . . While thou art pouring forth thy soul abroad/
In such an esctasy!'), that is, the out-pouring of the soul in
music is equated with death:

> When the great deity, for earth too ripe,
> Let his divinity o'er-flowing die
> In music, through vales of Thessaly . . .
>
> > > (I, 142–44)

Finally, the very rhymes of the last stanza of the ode ('. . .
toll me back from thee to my sole self! / Adieu! the fancy
cannot cheat so well / As she is famed to do, deceiving elf.'),
as well as the identical observation, occur in

> The journey homeward to habitual self!
> A mad pursuing of the fog-born elf,
> Cheats us . . .
>
> > > ("Endymion," II, 276–79)

Cross-reference is a mere curiosity if it does not serve to

indicate not merely habits of language, personal clichés, but habits of sensibility. I believe that the four passages cited above do indicate such a habit, exhibited in inflections of the pattern which receives a formal definition in the 'Ode to a Nightingale.' If we may accept them as so doing, we may expect to find resembling psychological contours, or the same contours differently articulated, in other poems. Even in 'I Stood Tip-Toe,' written probably in late 1816, almost two and a half years before the 'Ode,' occurs a subtle iteration both of the language and perceptional habit of the 'Ode':

A bush of May flowers . . .
And let long grass grow round the roots to
keep them
Moist, cool and green, and shade the violets . . .
(lines 29, 32–33)

Compare, in stanza v of the 'Ode,' 'mid-Mays eldest child' followed by the 'fast-fading violets cover'd up in leaves.' Moreover . . . the natural observation in both sets of lines— the covering of roots and violets—has its relationship, in so small detail, with the verduous covering which forms the general setting not only of this ode but also of other poems,— with a few exceptions, of all the poems that Keats wrote.[10]

Equally broad implications are found for another recurrent image achieving full expression in the Nightingale ode. David Perkins writes:

Like many of Keats's finest passages, the description of the 'draught of vintage' magnificently condenses a metaphor recurrent throughout his career. In 'To Charles Cowden Clarke' wine is metaphorically linked with poetry:

Because my wine was of too poor a savour
For one whose palate gladdens in the flavour
Of sparkling Helicon,
(lines 25–27)

---

10 *Ibid.*, pp. 31–32.

he has never 'penn'd a line' to Clarke, and in a prose passage he compares the 'pleasures of Song' to 'cups of old wine.' Near the beginning of *Endymion* 'All lovely tales that we have heard or read' are

> An endless fountain of immortal drink,
> Pouring unto us from the heaven's brink.
>   (lines 23–24)

In *Endymion* (III, 801), Keats speaks of 'a pure wine / Of happiness,' and wine is frequently associated with the ascent to what Keats termed 'heaven.' It makes man a Hermes, Keats said [*Letters,* II, 64], and in *Hyperion* Apollo cries that he is deified

> As if some blithe wine
> Or bright elixir peerless I had drunk,
> And so become immortal.
>   (III, 118–20)

And in *Lamia* wine 'has every soul from human trammels freed' (II, 210). Thus wine was at one time or another explicitly linked with poetry, with imagination, with happiness, with 'heaven,' in short with all that the nightingale represents.[11]

Perkins' analysis of the "Bright star" sonnet provides an example of how Keats manipulates the significations of his terms within a single poem, and he demonstrates that this manipulation is structural.

In the first line the star begins to represent the state to which man aspires. . . . Moreover, the star is eternal, sensuously aware ('watching'), and sleepless just as the poet would like to be. It is, however, alone and an 'eremite.' In this context, the patient eremite is one who does not experience human

---

[11] Perkins, pp. 248–49. See also Evert's development of this discovery in terms of Keats's aesthetic theories, pp. 67–72.

passions, having made a withdrawal for religious purposes. Hence the star watches the sea in its 'priest-like task / Of pure ablution' as it purifies 'Earth's human shores,' or the snow which, like the sea, seems to purify or at least hide the earth. The star, in other words, is part of an order of cold, chaste, pure, and eternal things—of sea, snow, and mountains —existing in an immense sweep of space, and this order is felt to be unresponsive or even unfriendly to earthly or human qualities which it seeks to purge or conceal. In contrast to this, the sestet describes a warm, sensual, and intimate human situation. Because the star almost immediately reveals aspects or characteristics which make it inadequate as a symbol, the poet begins his withdrawal from it at the same time that he takes it up ('Not in lone splendour . . .'). In the drama of the poem, he discovers that his wish is not to be like the star after all, but rather to transpose the potentiality of the star for eternal awareness into the realm of human life and feeling, and that of the most intense variety. Yet it might also be argued that the contrast in the sestet is not as thorough going as it may seem at first. By means of irrational and almost sub-liminal correspondences, feelings of religious purity associated with the star are partially carried into the sestet, modifying what might have been a wholly erotic situation.[12]

Properly the whole of Walter Evert's *Aesthetic and Myth in the Poetry of Keats* belongs in this section or else this study belongs in his book, for his methods of investigation are much the same as mine. I think that the most representative extract I can provide that will suffice to show his use of the method is the comparison of "Endymion," I, 710–end, with "La Belle Dame." (It will be remembered that I have already stated my support for Evert in his disputation with Wasserman on the subject of the knight's "weakness" and the faery child's "evil power," in chapter 8.)

In "Endymion"

we find the situation thus: the despondent Endymion has been

---

[12] *Ibid.*, pp. 232–33.

entreated by his sister Peona to confess the cause of his melancholy. Endymion has replied with an account of his first dream and of the sense of estrangement from the natural world with which it left him. After a pause, in which Peona meditates the best way to undertake a protest which she fears will be vain in any case, she gently upbraids Endymion. . . . [Here Evert quotes "Endymion," I, 721–760.]

The sum of Peona's argument is that Endymion has demeaned himself by forsaking the active life of valor for the pursuit of love, and more than that, for a love that is phantasmal, engendered in a sick fancy which has lost the ability to distinguish between dreams and reality. That Endymion's pursuit of the visionary goddess represents Keats's then-normal view of the imagination in pursuit of ultimate beauty and truth is implicit in the *form* of Peona's acknowledgement that Endymion's impulse is grounded in universal experience. Using the habitual Keatsian referents, she says that she too has been charmed by the sunset hour, has gazed upon the 'western cloudiness' and felt her imagination stirred by cloud shapes of 'gold rocks' and 'gold sands' and been led by these to splendid visions. The difference between her and Endymion is that she reckons this play of the fancy to be no more than just that, and does not wish to 'mount / into those regions,' thereby placing her affections and hopes for felicity in such fantasies. Endymion's pursuit of love, a love that 'doth scathe / The gentle heart, as northern blasts do roses,' and its displacement of the real world by a world of imagination, are thus characterized as pernicious.

> Stirred by this challenge, Endymion
rouses himself, and

> amid his pains
> He seem'd to taste a drop of manna-dew,
> Full palatable; and a colour grew
> Upon his cheek, while thus he lifeful spake.
> ("*Endymion*," I, 765–68)

What he speaks is the speech on 'fellowship with essence' in which he defends the authenticity of love and imagination as modes of achieving a 'self-destroying' spiritual reality which beggars that inferior kind centered in a consciousness of self-hood in the substantive world. Since he has the last word, Endymion is clearly to be taken as the winner of the argument.

In "La Belle Dame," on the other hand, we might say that Peona wins the argument. If we abstract the general characteristics of the situation, we find the *Endymion* episode and "La Belle Dame" to be identical. A man of valor (Endymion/ Knight at Arms) has been reduced to a state of dejection and torpor by an experience of perfect love (Endymion's dream/ knight's adventure) with a lady who proved to have no fixed existence in the world of substantial nature (moon-goddess/ belle dame). In addition to these radical similarities, the two poems share a number of lesser similarities. In both, the lady is wholly compliant, indeed, as much the aggressor as the man, (*End.*, I, 633–36, 653–57; 'Belle Dame,' 19–33). In both, the lovers move with their ladies from the place of meeting to a place of love making which is associated in its accompanying imagery with a mountain cavern (*End.*, I, 640–50; 'Belle Dame,' 21–22, 29). In both, after the fulfillment in kisses the man falls asleep (*End.*, I, 672–78; 'Belle Dame,' 33). In both, the disappointed lover is identified by paleness of complexion (*End.*, I, 627–28; 'Belle Dame,' 2, 9–12), and birds and roses are employed as images correlative with the lover's despondence. (*End.*, I, 698–703, 733–34; 'Belle Dame,' 4, 11–12). In both 'manna-dew' is associated with commitment to the experience (*End.*, I, 765–68; 'Belle Dame,' 26), in the former identified with the vigor which returns to Endymion when he defends his commitment, and in the latter used as an agency to induce commitment. There are other similarities but there is no need to press them. The argument does not depend upon an assumption of interchangeable symbolic equivalents but upon awareness of a common nexus of poetic elements which occur when, and indeed because, the poet's mind is engaged with the same essential problem. Given this fact, there remains one enormous difference between the poems: in *Endymion* the narrative experience is good; in 'La Belle Dame' it is evil.

The primary basis for this judgment is, of course, the conduct of the narratives themselves. Endymion is given the opportunity to justify his experiences, but nobody justifies the experience of the knight. Indeed, he is warned by the spirits of her past victims that he is in the evil power of an enchantress. Furthermore, Endymion's experience is not over. Although the power of his vision has temporarily estranged him from the world of nature, the narrative will go on to a reconciliation of the real and ideal worlds for Endymion, and to a pragmatic justification of Endymion's affirmative idealism. In the case of the woebegone knight, the poem ends with his enchantment still in force as he sits, emptied of all capacity for significant action and oblivious to the natural processes of the world around him, waiting for another experience of what we have every reason to suppose will never come to him again. He is, in fact, just what Peona said Endymion would become if he did not mend his imaginative ways, a heroic figure lost to valor, wasted by love, and so much in the grip of a malign fantasy and out of touch with the real world as to be hardly even sane.

Under the circumstances, I think it very hard not to infer as the theme of 'La Belle Dame' the anti-theme of its prototype in *Endymion*. In the light of what we have seen of Keats's shifting values between the two poems— of the rejection in the epistle to Reynolds of imagination as a guide to truth, and of the very real fear in 'God of the Meridian' and 'Lines Written in the Highlands after a Visit to Burn's Country,' that the spirit which leaves the world too far behind, in its flight toward ideal experience, hovers on the verge of madness—it is not too much to say that precisely what *Endymion* affirms and 'La Belle Dame' denies is the holiness of the heart's affections when they are made correlative with the truth of imagination.[13]

By examining all Keats's poetry and letters for recurrent figurative relationships, and by analyzing them in the order of their composition, this study supplements the work of the

---

[13] Evert, pp. 250–56.

scholars cited in the appendix. Because most of their work is concentrated on the major poetry, they have given us valuable insights into individual poems; but they have provided all too little interpretation of the bulk of Keats's poetry, they could not trace Keats's successive adoption of alternative attitudes toward major problems of life and art, and they have not developed a methodology capable of explicating poetry structured by its figurative relationships. The present study attempts to perform all these; and to my way of thinking, the most interesting and useful parts are the interpretations of Keats's less well known poetry, and the demonstration of the interdependence of all his poetry.

Bibliography

Abrams, Meyer H. *The Mirror and the Lamp*. New York, 1958.

Alexander, Peter. *Hamlet: Father and Son*. The Lord North-cliffe Lectures, University College, London, 1953. Oxford, 1955.

Armstrong, Edward A. *Shakespeare's Imagination: A Study of the Psychology of Association and Inspiration*. London, 1946.

Bate, Walter Jackson. *John Keats*. Cambridge, Mass., 1963.

Beyer, Werner W. *Keats and the Daemon King*. Oxford, 1946.

Blackstone, Bernard. *The Consecrated Urn: An Interpretation of Keats in terms of Growth and Form*. New York, 1959.

Brooks, Cleanth. "The Artistry of Keats," in *The Major English Romantic Poets: A Symposium in Reappraisal,* edited by Thorpe, Baker, and Weaver. Carbondale, Ill., 1957.

——. *The Well-Wrought Urn*. New York, 1947.

Brooks, Elmer. " 'The Poet' An Error in the Keats Canon." *MLN,* LXVII (Nov. 1952), 450–54.

Brown, Stephen J. *The World of Imagery: Metaphor and Kindred Imagery*. London, 1927.

Burke, Kenneth. *A Grammar of Motives*. New York, 1945.

——. *The Philosophy of Literary Form*. Baton Rouge, La., 1941.

Bush, Douglas. *John Keats: His Life and Writings*. New York, 1966.

Caldwell, James R. *John Keats' Fancy*. Ithaca, N. Y., 1945.

Colvin, Sir Sidney. *John Keats: his life and poetry, his friends, critics, and after-fame*. New York, 1917.

Croker, John Wilson. "Endymion: A Poetic Romance." *Quarterly Review,* XXXVII (April 1818), 204–8.

D'Avanzo, Mario. *Keats's Metaphors for the Poetic Imagination.* Durham, N.C., 1967.

Evert, Walter. *Aesthetic and Myth in the Poetry of Keats.* Princeton, N.J., 1965.

Fausset, Hugh I'A. *Keats: A Study in Development.* London, 1927.

Finney, Claude Lee. *The Evolution of Keats's Poetry.* 2 vols. Cambridge, Mass., 1936.

Fogle, Richard Harter. *The Imagery of Keats and Shelley.* Chapel Hill, N.C., 1949.

Ford, Newell F. *The Prefigurative Imagination of John Keats.* Palo Alto, Calif., 1951.

Garrod, H. W. *Keats.* London, 1926.

Gérard, Albert. "Coleridge, Keats, and the Modern Mind." *Essays in Criticism,* I (July 1951), 249–61.

———. "Romance and Reality: Continuity and Growth in Keats's View of Art." *K-SJ,* XI (Winter 1962), 17–29.

Gittings, Robert. *John Keats: The Living Year.* London, 1954.

———. *The Mask of Keats.* London, 1960.

Goldberg, M. A. "The Fears of John Keats." *MLQ,* XVIII (June 1957), 125–31.

Havens, R. D. "Unreconciled Opposites in Keats." *PQ,* XIV (Oct. 1935), 289–300.

Jeffrey, Francis. "Review of Endymion, Lamia, Etc." *The Edinburgh Review,* XXXIV (August 1820), 203–13.

Keats, John. *The Complete Poetry and Selected Prose.* Edited by H. E. Briggs. New York, 1951.

———. *Keats' Poetical Works.* Edited by H. W. Garrod. 2nd ed. Oxford, 1958.

———. *The Letters of John Keats.* Edited by Hyder Rollins. 2 vols. Cambridge, Mass., 1958.

———. *The Poems of John Keats.* Edited by E. DeSelincourt, 5th ed. London, 1961.

———. *The Poetical Works and Other Writings of John Keats.*

Edited by Harry Buxton Forman, revised by Maurice Buxton Forman (Hampstead Edition), 8 vols., 1938–1939.

Lowell, Amy. *John Keats.* 2 vols. Boston and New York, 1925.

Mahoney, John L. "Keats and The Metaphor of Fame." *ES,* XLIV (Oct. 1963), 355–57.

Murry, John M. *Countries of the Mind.* 2nd Series. Oxford, 1931.

————. *Keats.* London, 1955.

Ormerod, David. "Nature's Eremite: Keats and the Liturgy of Passion." *K-SJ,* XVI (1967), 71–77.

Perkins, David. "Keats's Odes and Letters: Recurrent Diction and Imagery." *K-SJ,* II (Jan. 1953), 51–60.

————. *The Quest for Permanence: The Symbolism of Wordsworth, Shelley, and Keats.* Cambridge, Mass., 1959.

Pettet, E. C. *On The Poetry of Keats.* New York, 1957.

Richards, Ivor Armstrong. *The Philosophy of Rhetoric.* New York, 1936.

Ridley, M. R. *Keats' Craftsmanship: A Study in Poetic Development.* Oxford, 1933.

Russell, Stanley. " 'Self-Destroying' Love in Keats." *K-SJ,* XVI (1967), 77–91.

Slote, Bernice. *Keats and The Dramatic Principle.* Lincoln, Nebr., 1958.

Steele, Mabel. "The Authorship of 'The Poet' and Other Sonnets." *K-SJ,* V (1956), 69–80.

Stekel, Wilhelm. *Auto-Erotism: A Psychiatric Study of Onanism and Neurosis.* Translated by James S. Van Teslaar. New York, 1961.

Spurgeon, Caroline. *Shakespeare's Imagery and What It Tells Us.* Cambridge, 1935.

Stillinger, Jack. "The Hoodwinking of Madeline: Scepticism in 'The Eve of St. Agnes.' " *SP,* LVIII (July 1961), 535–55.

Teich, Nathaniel. "Criticism and Keats's *Grecian Urn.*" *PQ,* XLIV (Oct. 1965), 496–502.

Thorpe, Clarence DeWitt. *The Mind of John Keats.* New York, 1926.

Trilling, Lionel. "The Poet as Hero: The Letters of John Keats." *Cornhill Magazine,* CLXV (Autumn 1951), 281–302.

Van Ghent, Dorothy. "Image Types and Antithetical Structures in the Work of Keats." Ph.D. dissertation, University of California, 1942.

Visick, Mary. " 'Tease us out of thought': Keats's *Epistle to Reynolds* and the Odes." *K-SJ,* XV (1966), 87–98.

Ward, Aileen, *John Keats: The Making of A Poet.* New York, 1963.

Wasserman, Earl. *The Finer Tone: Keats' Major Poems.* Baltimore, 1953.

———. "Keats' Sonnet 'The Poet,' " *MLN,* LXVII (Nov. 1952), 454–56.

Whitley, Alvin. "The Autograph of Keats's 'In Drear Nighted December.' " *HLB,* V (Winter 1951), 116–22.

Wigod, Jacob D. "Keats's Ideal in the 'Ode on a Grecian Urn.' " *PMLA,* LXXII (March 1957), 113–21.

Wimsatt, William K. Jr., *The Verbal Icon: Studies in the Meaning of Poetry.* Kentucky, 1954.

Acknowledgments

Grateful acknowledgement is herewith made to the following for permission to quote from the books listed below.

Archon Books for permission to quote from Hugh I. A. Fausset, *Keats: A Study in Development* (Hamden, Conn.: The Shoe String Press Inc., 1966). Reprinted by permission of Archon Books.

Barnes & Noble, Incorporated, and Heinemann Educational Books Ltd., for permission to reprint from R. Gittings, *John Keats: The Living Year* (London: Heinemann Educational Books Ltd., 1954).

The Belknap Press of Harvard University Press for permission to reprint from Walter J. Bate, *John Keats* (Cambridge, Mass.: Belknap Press, 1963).

Ernest Benn Limited for permission to reprint from Edward A. Armstrong, *Shakespeare's Imagination: A Study of the Psychology of Association and Inspiration* (London: Ernest Benn Ltd., 1946).

Cambridge University Press for permission to reprint from E. C. Pettet, *On the Poetry of Keats* (New York: Cambridge University Press, 1957), and for permission to reprint from Caroline Spurgeon, *Shakespeare's Imagery and What It Tells Us* (New York: Cambridge, 1935).

The Clarendon Press, Oxford, for permission to quote from H. W. Garrod's Oxford English Texts edition of *The Poetical Works of John Keats* (2nd Edition, 1958) (London: The Clarendon Press, Oxford). Reprinted by permission of the Clarendon Press, Oxford.

232]

Cornell University Press for permission to reprint from James Caldwell: *John Keats' Fancy*. Copyright 1945 by Cornell University. Used by permission of Cornell University Press.

Farrar, Straus & Giroux, Inc. and The Society of Authors as literary representatives of the Estate of John Middleton Murry, for permission to reprint from John M. Murry, *Keats* (London: Jonathan Cape Ltd., 1955).

Harcourt Brace and World for permission to reprint from Cleanth Brooks, *The Well-Wrought Urn* (New York: Harcourt, Brace & World, 1947).

Harvard University Press for permission to reprint from Claude L. Finney, *The Evolution of Keats' Poetry* (Cambridge, Mass.: Harvard U. Press, 1936), and for permission to reprint from H. Rollins, ed., *The Letters of John Keats* (Cambridge, Mass.: Harvard U. Press, 1958), and for permission to reprint from David Perkins, *The Quest for Permanence: The Symbolism of Wordsworth, Shelley, and Keats* (Cambridge, Mass.: Harvard U. Press, 1959).

Heinemann Educational Books Ltd. for permission to reprint from R. Gittings, *The Mask of Keats* (London: Heinemann Educational Books Ltd., 1960).

Houghton Mifflin Company for permission to reprint from Amy Lowell, *John Keats* (Boston and New York: Houghton Mifflin Company, 1925).

The Johns Hopkins Press for permission to reprint from Earl Wasserman, *The Finer Tone: Keats' Major Poems* (Baltimore: The Johns Hopkins Press, 1953).

Liveright Publishing Corporation for permission to reprint from *Auto-Erotism* by Dr. Wilhelm Stekel. Permission of Liveright, Publishers, New York. Copyright 1950 by Liveright Publishing Corp.

Longmans Green & Co. Ltd. for permission to reprint from Bernard Blackstone, *The Consecrated Urn: An Interpretation of Keats in terms of Growth and Form* (London: Longmans Green & Co. Ltd., 1959).

Index of Titles

Index of Authors

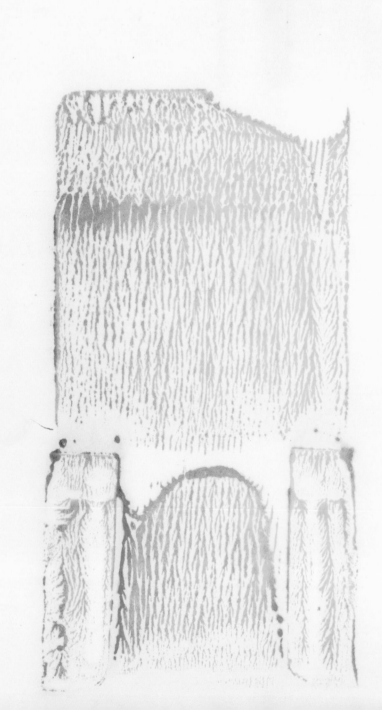